Using Microsoft® Report Builder

A Microsoft Office Report Authoring
Environment for SQL Server and Other Data

by

Robert S. Bussom

Table of Contents

Preface

This short book about creating and distributing reports based on SQL Server and other data is essentially an improved chapter or so from my book, <u>Data Analysis and Data Mining using Microsoft Business Intelligence Tools: Excel, Access, and Report Builder with SQL Server</u>, available on <u>Amazon</u> in print and eBook formats and on the Barnes and Noble Nook. I thought that I should provide this excerpt for those interested in Report Builder only and not necessarily the whole Microsoft business intelligence (BI) enchilada. You may see more information about BI and my book on my Website <u>www.zerobits.info</u>.

The content is intended for people who are knowledgeable about and comfortable with desktop applications, especially those by Microsoft, on Windows-based computers, and who have a need and interest in preparing reports using SQL Server and other data for themselves and others. The book includes a brief overview of BI that may be skipped without much damage and discusses how to create reports using Report Builder to publish on and distribute with the SQL Server Report Server.

After memorizing the book in minute detail, the reader will be able to use the SQL Server Report Manager and Report Builder to create, publish, and distribute sophisticated standard and ad hoc reports that can include drill-down and drill-through capabilities, charts and gauges, key performance indicators, Databars, and Sparklines for dashboard-like presentations. I took a guided tour approach to the topics in the book, and I've tried to provide explanations as appropriate to help you understand what's going on so that you can generalize beyond examples and screen shots, of which there are many.

My original book published in August 2102 was based on SQL Server 2008 R2 Release 2 (a sort of a midlife update). Since that time SQL Server 2012 has ben released, but Report Builder 3.0 (RB3) used for the original book has not been updated as far as I know. You may download RB3 for SQL Server 2012 at

<u>http://www.microsoft.com/en-us/download/details.aspx?id=29072</u>.

Just search the Internet for other versions for SQL Server.

Preface

I hope that you find book useful. Suggestions for improvement of the book and Website are encouraged and appreciated. Please email me at bussom@zerobits.info or use the Contact Us page at www.zerobits.info. Thanks.

Chapter 1 - Introduction to Business Intelligence Microsoft Style

To me Business intelligence (BI) is a set of concepts, methods, and computer related technologies used to transform an organization's data into information to enhance operational and strategic decision making. BI applications include data warehousing, online analytical processing, data and statistical analysis, forecasting, data mining, and reporting.

This definition emphasizes the transformation of data into information. It specifically recognizes that BI is used for operational as well as strategic decision making whereas the early approaches to BI seemed to focus on executive-level information needs. It also incorporates computer technologies without which BI would not be possible. It avoids reference to decision support systems as that term has expanded in generality and ambiguity, and it focuses on the organization's data which the organization routinely captures and stores, intentionally understating acquisition and analysis of data related to factors external to the organization such as would be implied by terms like "military intelligence" and "competitive intelligence."

Furthermore, it broadens the scope of BI beyond larger business and enterprises to be useful for organizations in general of all types and sizes. In the context of this book the term "business data" refers to the business of the organization whether it be commerce, government, education, not-for-profit, or whatever.

A Generic Business Intelligence Model

The intention of BI is to take a business's raw data, possibly from a variety of disparate sources, convert it into relevant, usable data and information, and transmit and present it to appropriate users. Most of the data sources in Figure 1-1 below should be familiar to you. The BI processes may be as simple as an Excel worksheet on the desktop for a single user or as complex as the full use of the Microsoft SQL Server BI package at the enterprise level.

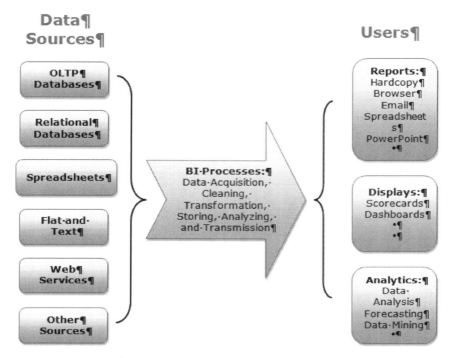

Figure 1-1 Generic BI Model

Reports

Users may receive reports from the BI processes in a variety of forms including hardcopy (ugh!), on the organization's intranet or directly from SQL Server's Reporting Services with a browser, or pushed via email. BI reports follow a conventional report format by presenting data in an organized way perhaps including some data visualization such as charts or graphs. BI reports are similar to traditional hardcopy reports and may be static like the one in Figure 1-2 or more dynamic interactive reports with filter and drill-down capabilities and graphics as shown by the one in Figure 1-3 from the Microsoft AdventureWorks Sample Reports application.

FoodMart Store Sales

Store	Quarter (Store Sales)				
	Q1	Q2	Q3	Q4	Total
1	15,063	12,302	12,756	16,276	56,397
2	1,061	1,118	1,151	1,449	4,780
3	13,482	14,064	13,158	17,277	57,982
4	15,378	13,542	12,107	13,839	54,865
5	1,357	1,247	1,035	1,264	4,903
6	12,470	10,558	14,357	14,980	52,365
Total	58,811	52,831	54,565	65,085	231,291

Figure 1-2 Simple Static Report

The report in Figure 1-2 was created quickly using the Report Builder capability of Microsoft's Reporting Services from a cleaned up, upgraded version of the old FoodMart database included as an example, I believe, in SQL Server 2000.

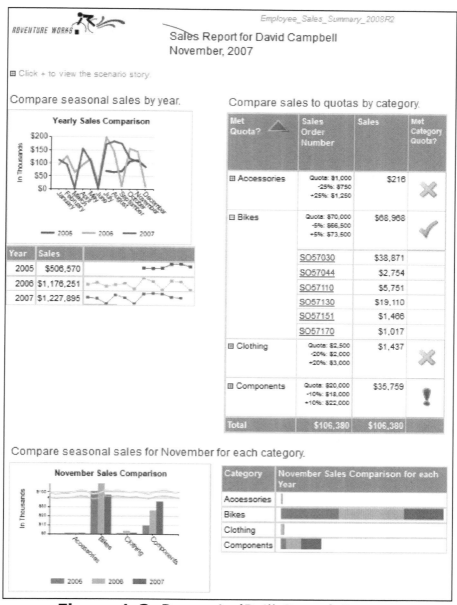

Figure 1-3 Dynamic (Drill-Down) Report

Notice the plus (+) and minus (-) buttons in the AdventureWorks sample report in Figure 1-3 which allows users to expand a section of the report to a lower level of detail. For example, the +

button has been clicked to expand the Bikes product category to list product subcategories. This interactive process is called drilling-down. Hyperlinks to other reports as well as charts and graphs can be added to reports.

Displays

Data and information displays, primarily dashboards and scorecards, are different from reports. They are created to present a visual representation of the current status of processes and projects in the case of dashboards or of performance against some benchmark in the case of scorecards. Dashboards and scorecards are usually associated with executive-level managers but there is no reason that they cannot be used effectively by the rest of us. The differences between dashboards and scorecards are essentially unimportant, and in practice dashboards and scorecards usually are intermixed in a display.

Figure 1-4 shows a representative dashboard from MicroStrategy, an independent BI software provider. Notice how this image presents current performance, i.e., the dashboard is descriptive. In comparison the scorecard from Dashboards By Example shown in Figure 1-5 shows actual performances compared with target performance, i.e., the scorecard is evaluative.

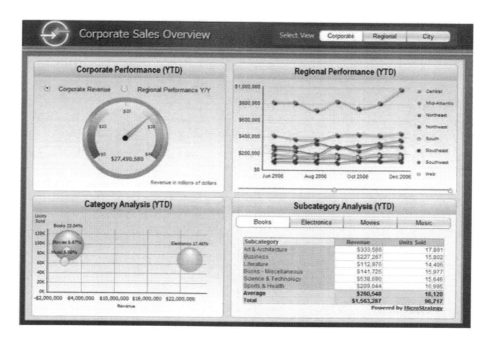

Figure 1-4 Example Dashboard from MicroStrategy

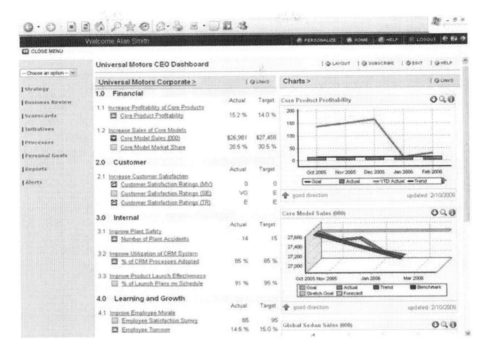

Figure 1-5 Example Scorecard from Dashboards By Example

Regardless of whether the display is called a dashboard or scorecard it presents a considerable amount information in a single visual representation, as in the hackneyed expression, a picture is worth a thousand words. Display designers must take care to represent data fairly in displays. Managers may make decisions based on these displays, and performance unintentionally misrepresented may lead to unintended consequences.

Analytics

In BI analytics we're talking about tools, methods, and models that help us extract information from the business's data. It helps us identify patterns and anomalies; It stimulates us to pose questions about business processes and strategies and to answer them; And it serves as the foundation for models that assist in decision making.

In our generic BI model analytics includes data analysis, forecasting, and data mining. Data analysis can be an umbrella term covering all types of methods and models including quantitative data analysis, qualitative data analysis, exploratory data analysis, statistical analysis, forecasting, data mining, and so on. We use data analysis to mean those methods, procedures, and models other than forecasting and data mining techniques that are relevant for understanding and using business data.

Business Intelligence Processes

Figure 1-1 lists data acquisition, cleansing, transformation, storing, analysis, and transmission as the major BI processes that get data from sources to users. We'll explore the BI processes only a bit here. Figure 1-6 presents a simplified generic diagram of BI architecture.

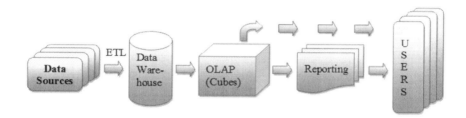

Figure 1-6 Simplified Generic BI Architecture

Original data, usually online transaction processing (OLTP) data, are loaded into a data warehouse by extract, transform, and load (ETL) processes. Online analytical processing (OLAP) transforms these data in the warehouse into a multidimensional database. In the main path of the architecture above the reporting service utilizes the multidimensional data to produce reports for users. In the upper path users may access the multidimensional database directly for analysis, presentation, and data mining.

A multidimensional database can be envisioned as a multidimensional object with dimensions on the axes and measures as cell values. In BI this object is called a cube although it may have more than three dimensions. Figure 1-7 below shows a three dimensional cube example with Product, Customer, and Time as dimensions and sales as the cell values.

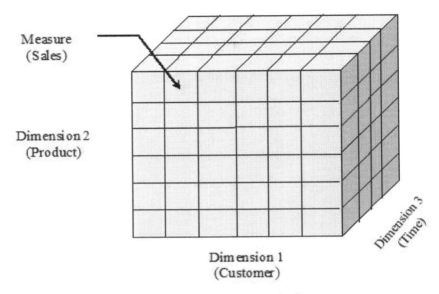

Figure 1-7 OLAP Cube

You can think of a multidimensional database as a stack of tables like the one in Figure 1-8. Here, Products and Customers are the row and column headings with sales in dollars in the intersecting cells. Each table contains sales for one day on the time dimension. In the example total sales for Product 5 to Customer 3 on April 5 were $274.61.

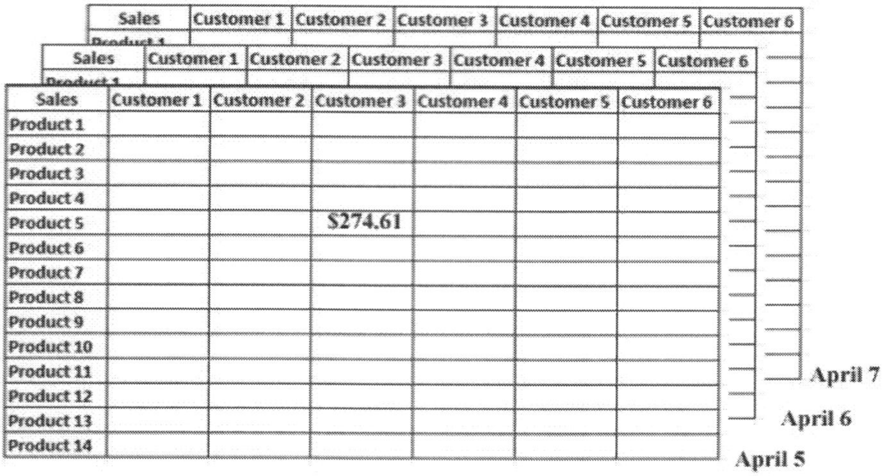

Sales	Customer 1	Customer 2	Customer 3	Customer 4	Customer 5	Customer 6
Product 1						
Product 2						
Product 3						
Product 4						
Product 5			$274.61			
Product 6						
Product 7						
Product 8						
Product 9						
Product 10						
Product 11						
Product 12						
Product 13						
Product 14						

April 7
April 6
April 5

Figure 1-8 OLAP Cube as Stacked Tables

OLAP performs queries very quickly because some of the data for queries are preprocessed at the time the data are loaded into the multidimensional database. In addition OLAP may aggregate fact values at higher levels of consolidation in advance. For example, OLAP may aggregate sales by week, month, quarter, and year. Thus, when a user requests, say, total sales for each product for the month of April, OLAP already has the values available and does not have to compute them from atomic-level data.

SQL Server

In a nutshell SQL Server has four main components: a Database Engine, Analysis Services, Integration Services, and Reporting Services: the Database Engine creates and manages SQL Server databases; Analysis Services is used to create and deploy cubes and data mining structures and models; Integration Services is used to extract, transform, and load data from various sources into SQL Server databases; and Reporting Services is a full-featured application for report creation and management to design, modify, store, and publish reports. You can schedule report processing, distribute reports according to a schedule, and build ad hoc reports. For the purpose of this book we will only explore Reporting Services in more detail. But first, because we utilize AdventureWorks data in many examples, we briefly introduce it below.

AdventureWorks

AdventureWorks is a collection of SQL Server samples and examples provided by Microsoft. Sample databases are no longer installed automatically with SQL Server - they must be downloaded from CodePlex and installed separately. Adventure Works, a hypothetical company, sells bicycles that it manufactures and related products such as clothing, components, and accessories that it purchases to consumers online and to stores for resale. It is an international company with sales in North America, Europe, and Australia and its corporate headquarters in Washington state with regional sales teams located in their primary markets. The Adventure Works OLTP database containing data related to customers, human resources, production, purchasing, and sales is the data source for the AdventureWorks DW (data warehouse) and AdventureWorks Cube.

SQL Server Reporting Services

Reporting Services is accessed via Visual Studio in SQL Server 2012 or the Business Intelligence Development Studio (BIDS), a Visual Studio add-in, in earlier versions of SQL Server. Reporting Services uses the Report Definition Language (RDL) to define reports, i.e., reports are saved to .rdl files. A report definition contains data retrieval and layout information for a report. RDL is composed of XML elements that match an XML grammar created for Reporting Services.

There are two types of basic reports available in the Reporting Services: tabular and matrix. Tabular reports display lists of data in columns whereas matrix reports are like cross tabulations, i.e., fields (dimension attributes) appear is both rows and columns with values (measures) in the cell intersections.

For just a peek at Reporting Services Figure 1-9 is a screen shot of report layout in Visual Studio Reporting Services design view. The data source, the AdventureWorks Cube, is listed in the Solution Explorer in the right upper panel as well as the two reports that have been constructed in the project so far: the primary report, Sales by Product, and a subreport, Gross Profit

Margin by Product. The Toolbox in the left lower panel shows the objects that can be dragged and dropped onto the design surface. There are seven objects on the design surface: a textbox for the report title, Sales by Product; an image of the AdventureWorks logo that I copied from the AdventureWorks report samples; a matrix directly below the report title that presents data for Internet sales by product category and subcategory; a subreport container (the grey rectangle); a graph; a gauge, and a textbox for the gauge. The objects in the report are configured and formatted with menus and by setting various properties.

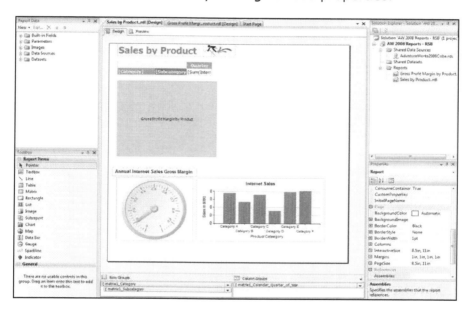

Figure 1-9 Reporting Services Design View

Figure 1-10 shows this report in preview view, i.e., how the report will actually appear. Now you can see the matrix-type tables for sales and gross profit margin that were shown as layouts in design view. A few comments about the report are in order. First, I constructed the report only to demonstrate the use of some of the tools available not to present a professional looking, useable report. I just dropped objects onto the design surface and did a little formatting and tinkering.

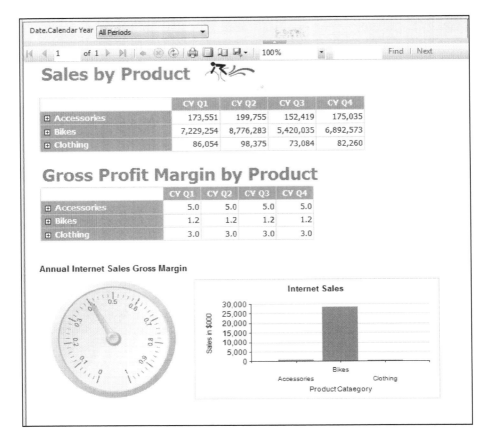

Figure 1-10 Reporting Services Preview View

Second, the primary report has a filter for selecting the year(s) to present in the report which is accomplished by including a parameter in the query that underlies the report. Figure 1-11a shows the Report Data tab that you can barely see in the upper left panel of Figure 1-9. In addition to listing the data used in the report, SalesDataset and GaugeDataset, the Report Data panel shows the parameters in the report. In this case the only parameter specified is the DateCalendarYear field. If we click on the filter selection area in the upper left corner beside the parameter name, Date.Calendar Year, in the Design panel in Figure 1-9, the listbox shown in Figure 1-11b would drop-down where we can select the year(s) to display. There "All Periods" is selected which displays the data for all periods combined. To select other years deselect "All Periods" and click the years to select.

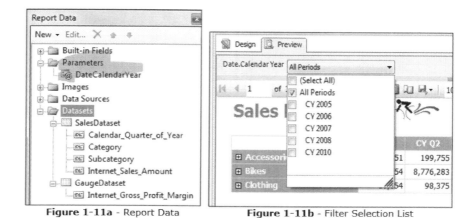

Figure 1-11a - Report Data   Figure 1-11b - Filter Selection List

Figure 1-11 Report Filter Example

Third, the subreport, Gross Profit Margin by Product is linked to the calendar year parameter in the primary report so when a year is selected for the primary report, the secondary report changes as well. Fourth, the two matrix-type tables are set up with drill-down capabilities as shown Figure 1-12 with the Accessories subcategory expanded in the Sales by Product table and the Bikes category expanded in the Gross Profit Margin by Product subreport table.

Fifth, it's possible to add drill-through capabilities to reports. A drill-through is similar to a hyperlink that uses textboxes or images as buttons to navigate to other reports, bookmarks, or URLs. Our discussion in the chapter about the Report Builder includes an example of drill-through.

Last, with the use of graphs, gauges, and tables reports can simulate dashboard and scorecard presentations. In fact, if the data source for the report is an Analysis Services cube, then Key Performance Indicators (KPIs) can be added to reports just like in dashboards and scorecards.

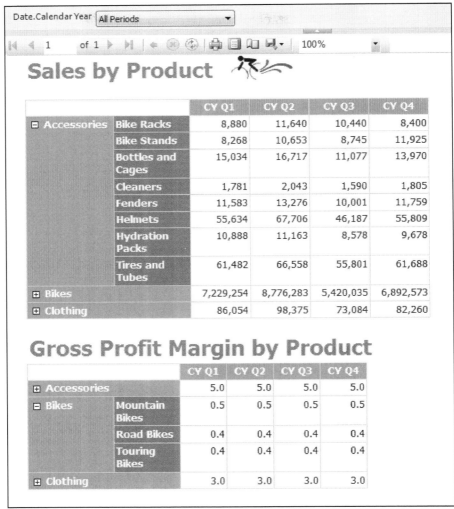

Figure 1-12 Drill-Down Example

Report Manager and Report Builder 3.0

Reports created in Reporting Services are made available to users through the SQL Server Report Server. Figure 1-13 shows my conceptualization of the Report Server architecture. The Report Server has access to about any data sources available and it manages a Report Server database. There are two sources for reports: those created by a developer using Reporting Services in SQL Server and those created by users using the Report Builder.

Users use a browser to interact with the Report Manager and use Report Builder, a Windows application, to create reports. In SQL Server 2005 the Report Server ran under Internet Information Services (IIS), the Windows Web server. Now, Reporting Services 2008 and beyond handle HTTP requests themselves so that IIS is no longer required for it. In SQL Server 2008 the Report Server included Report Builder 1.0, a Microsoft Office-like application to design reports. Report Builder has been updated to Report Builder 3.0 available by download from Microsoft.

In Chapter 2 we will explore the Report Manager and then learn how to use Report Builder 3.0 in Chapter 3.

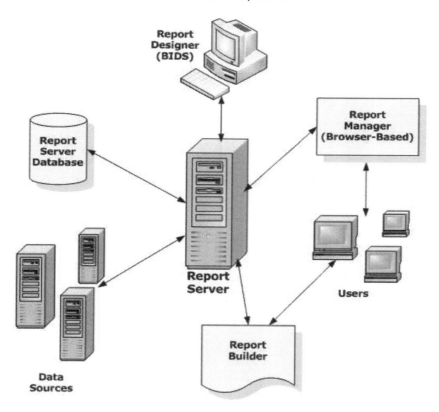

Figure 1-13 Report Server Architecture

Chapter 2 - Report Manager

As we learned in Chapter 1 a developer using SQL Server Reporting Services creates and manages reports using the Report Designer in Visual Studio or BIDS depicted at the top of Figure 1-13. There, the developer can also deploy (publish) the report to the Report Server for users to access. Deployment is an automated process initiated by the developer by selecting deploy from a project's menu. If the deployment is successful, the report will then show up in the list of available reports on the Report Server.

The Report Manager, the Report Server's user interface, is accessed in a browser at a URL something like http://<servername>/Reports. Of course, Internet Explorer as a Microsoft product renders the Report Manager's pages accurately. However, using other browsers may be problematic. In Firefox try the IE Tab add-on.

Figure 2-1 shows a partial screen shot of the Report Manager home page using the URL http://MAINGEAR/Reports for my setup. MAINGEAR is the name of the server on my local machine and Reports refers to the Report Manager. You are probably not hosting SQL Server on your local machine unless you are working with the Developer edition so ask the IT folks for the URL for your Report Server. Note that the availability of the various capabilities in the Report Manager depends on the permissions granted to the user. For example, some users may only view reports whereas others may create and publish reports.

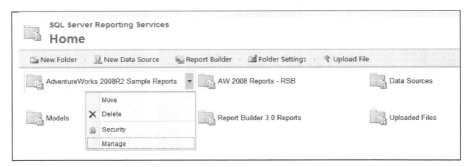

Figure 2-1 Report Manager in Internet Explorer

Objects available from the Report Manager are organized in a usual folder structure. You may perform operations on a folder by clicking the down arrow on the right which displays the box as shown in the figure for the AdventureWorks 2008R2 Sample Reports folder. In this example there are six folders. The first, the AdventureWorks Sample Reports folder, contains nine reports deployed from the Reporting Services AdventureWorks sample project downloaded from Microsoft. Figure 2-2 shows the contents of that folder, and Figure 2-3 shows part of the second report in the list, Employee Sales Summary 2008R2, which we saw a version of in Figure 1-12.

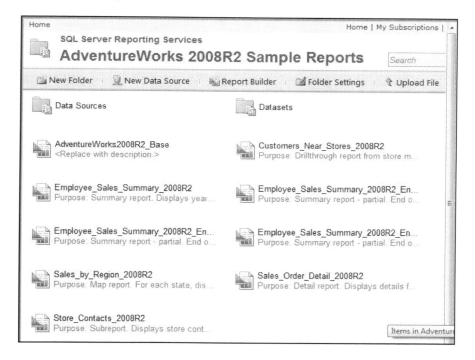

Figure 2-2 AdventureWorks Sample Reports Folder

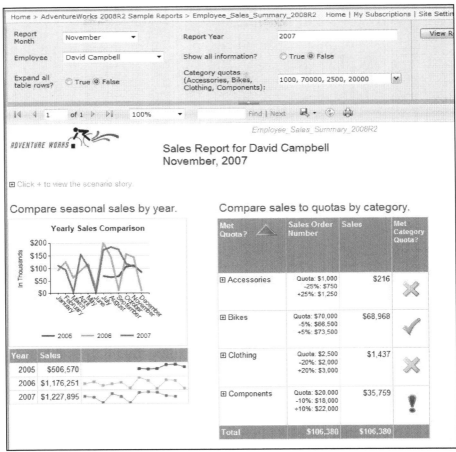

Figure 2-3 AdventureWorks Sample Report

The AW 2008 Reports - RSB and the Report Builder 3.0 folders listed in Figure 2-1 contain reports that I created, deploying reports from Reporting Services for the former folder and using Report Builder 3.0 for the latter. Data Sources, Models, and Uploaded Files are special folders that we'll get to shortly.

New Folder

Creating a new folder is about the same as creating one on a Windows computer. Figure 2-4 shows a screen shot of the New Folder window. To create a new folder just specify a name, an optional description, and click OK. Folders can be nested as usual.

To create a folder within a folder just navigate to the parent folder and click New Folder.

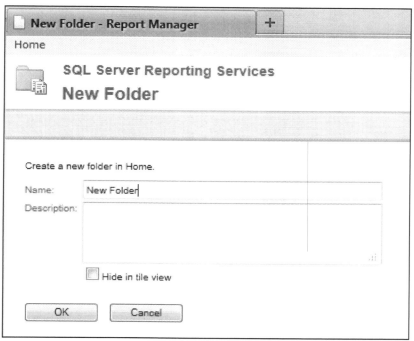

Figure 2-4 New Folder Window in Report Manager

Data Sources

The Data Sources folder contain (surprise!) data sources. These data sources are used by the Report Builder to build reports with a shared data source. More on that in a bit. Three data sources are available in my Data Sources folder in Figure 2-5: The AdventureWorks OLTP database, the DW database, and the Analysis Services Cube. To create a new data source click on the New Data Source menu item to access the Data Sources properties page shown in Figure 2-6 which shows the data source properties for the AdventureWorks2008Cube: its name; the data source type, an analysis Services cube in this case, and the connection string. The connection string will usually be of the form:

    data source=<SQL Server instance>;initial catalog=
        <source name>

In this example the server on my local machine is named MAINGEAR and the source is the cube from "Adventure Works DW 2008R2." Figure 2-7 displays a partial list of data source types available. Since the data source is a cube, the Microsoft SQL Server Analysis Services type is selected. The type of authentication credentials required to assess the data source is specified in the Connect using area. This example uses Windows integrated security.

Figure 2-5 Data Sources Folder

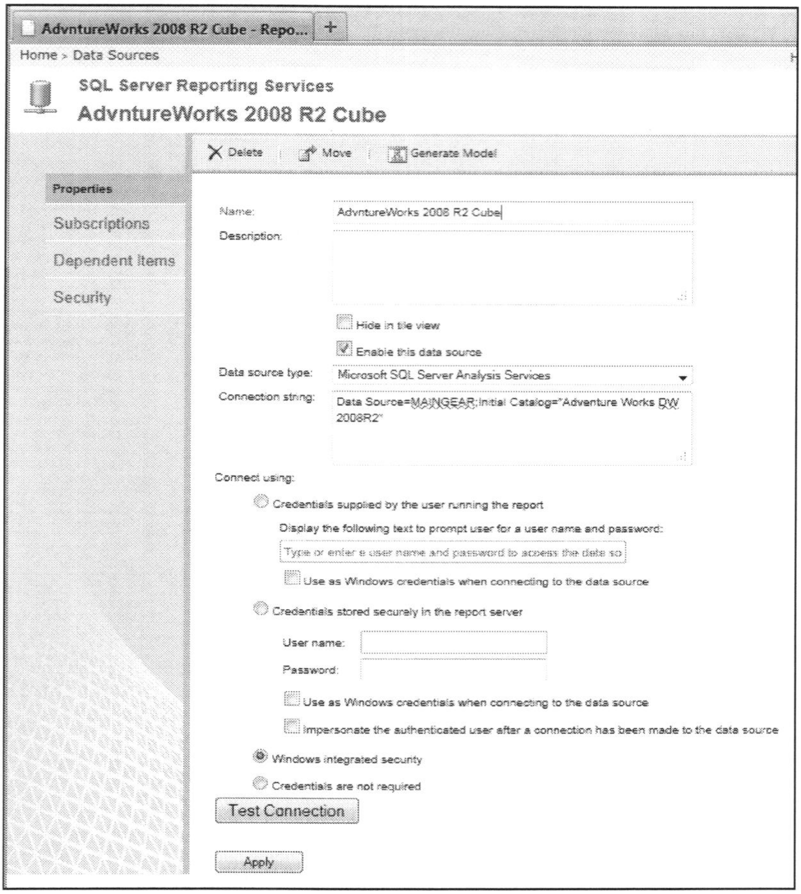

Figure 2-6 Data Sources Window

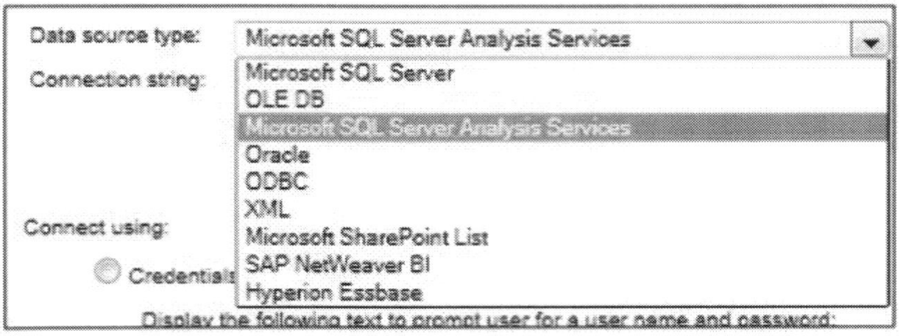

Figure 2-7 Data Source Types

Models

The Models folder in Figure 2-1 contains the list of data models available on the Report Server. In our case there is only one model listed, Adventureworks2008DW (not shown in a figure). Data models are representations of an underlying database that include relationships and queries. A data model created by a developer or database administrator can be used by Report Manager users as data sources for reports. This avoids the need for users to create a data source as discussed above.

Upload File

The Upload File menu action, of course, uploads a file to the Report Server and makes it available in the Report Manager. The usual file uploaded is a RDL file, i.e., a file containing a report definition prepared in Reporting Services, Report Builder, or some other application using the Report Definition Language (RDL). Other file types can be uploaded as well such as report model files (Semantic Model Definition Language - .smdl), images, or just about anything else. All files uploaded except RDL and SMDL files are stored as resources for the user or developer. For example I uploaded two files into a new folder called Uploaded Files: a jpeg image of the AdventureWorks logo and a Microsoft Word document. A partial screen shot of the Uploaded Files folder is shown in Figure 2-8a, and a view of the jpg file by clicking on its name is shown in Figure 2-8b.

Figure 2-8a - Uploaded File List

Figure 2-8b - Uploaded File View

Figure 2-8 Uploaded Files Example

Folder Settings

Within a folder clicking on Folder Settings in the action bar will display the folder properties window as shown for the AdventureWorks 2008R2 Sample Reports folder in Figure 2-9 where you may change the folder name and description as well as delete or move the folder.

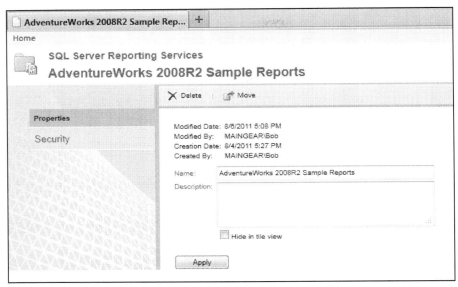

Figure 2-9 Folder Properties

Show Details

The Details View action on the far right of the menu area in Figure 2-1 is used to display object properties and to edit the properties or delete or move the objects. Figure 2-10 shows the detailed view of the Home page by clicking on the Details View button. Each row in the list represents an object on the page or folder. You may perform operation on a folder by using the drop down listbox as noted above.

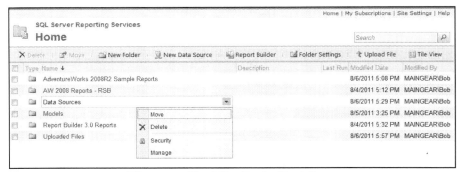

Figure 2-10 Details View

Clicking on the folder icon in the Type column in Figure 2-10 just lists the contents in the folder. Clicking on the check box in row enables the Delete and Move actions in the menu area. Clicking on Delete does just that. Clicking on Move opens the Move window in Figure 2-11. At the top of the window the object to move is identified, in this case the AdventureWorks 2008R2 Sample Reports folder. Below that the textbox indicates the location the object will be moved to, and the directory tree on the right allows the user to select the new location as I did here with the Data Sources folder. Note that the folders in the directory tree can be expanded as usual.

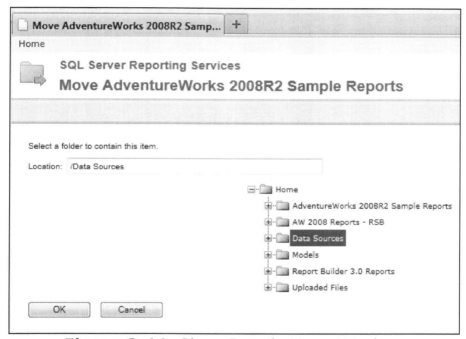

Figure 2-11 Show Details Move Window

Export and Print

You may export reports in a variety of formats. Figure 2-12 shows a partial screen shot of a Sales Report where I clicked the small disk icon to display the export options. If you want to export the report to Microsoft Word, then just select Word in the list and then click Export. A dialog box will open asking if you want to open or save the file. Proceed from there as usual. The application that supports the format, e.g., Microsoft Word, must be available. Note that reports with interactive features like drill-down probably won't work in exported reports. Use the printer icon to print the report in a similar manner.

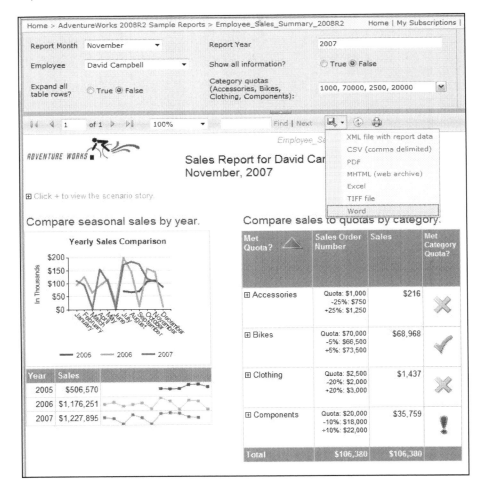

Figure 2-12 Report View Export Options

Subscriptions

Instead of viewing reports with the Report Manager users may receive reports via email or a Windows file share. A subscription is created by selecting the Subscribe option in the drop down menu for a particular report as in Figure 2-13. This will open the Subscription page shown in Figure 2-14.

(Tip: you may receive an error message something like "subscription cannot be created because the credentials used to run the report are not stored . . . ." This may be because the data source for the report must be using stored credentials. To remedy this go to the data source for the specific report. In Properties select Credentials stored securely in the report server. Enter a user name and password, check Use as Windows credentials when connecting to the data source, test the connection, and Apply.)

Figure 2-13 Report in the View Tab

Configuring the Subscription page is straightforward. Select the Delivered by mode, either email or Windows file share (if a file share is available). Fill in the recipient(s) information, select a delivery schedule by clicking on the Select Schedule button, and configure parameter values if parameters are available in the report. Clicking the Select Schedule button brings up the Schedule Details page shown in Figure 2-15 which is self-explanatory. The only parameter in this report is calendar year which is now set to All Periods, i.e., the data presented in the report will be the sum of all years. You could select one or more years for the report by using the listbox.

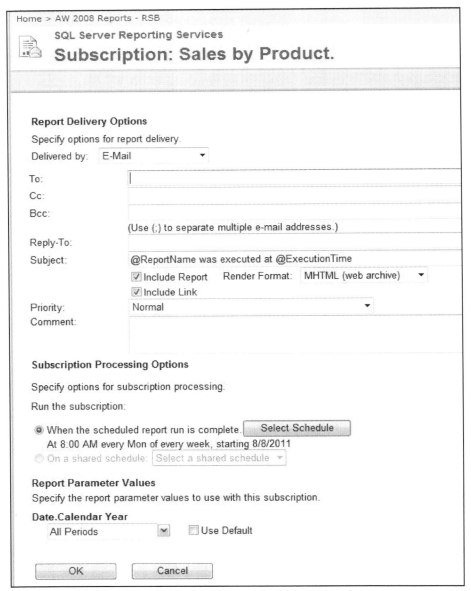

Figure 2-14 Subscription Window

Clicking OK to back out of the forms will return you to the report's subscription page as shown in Figure 2-15 which lists the new subscription. (By the way I successfully emailed this report to myself via my ISP.) You can also create a data-driven subscription as indicated by the New Data-driven Subscription action on the menu area in Figure 2-16 which is accessed by selecting Manage from the report options menu and then the Subscriptions tab. Data-driven subscriptions distribute reports to a recipient pool specified in a subscriber database. While configuration of data - driven subscriptions is beyond the scope of this book, information and tutorials are available about this in SQL Server Books Online and on the Web.

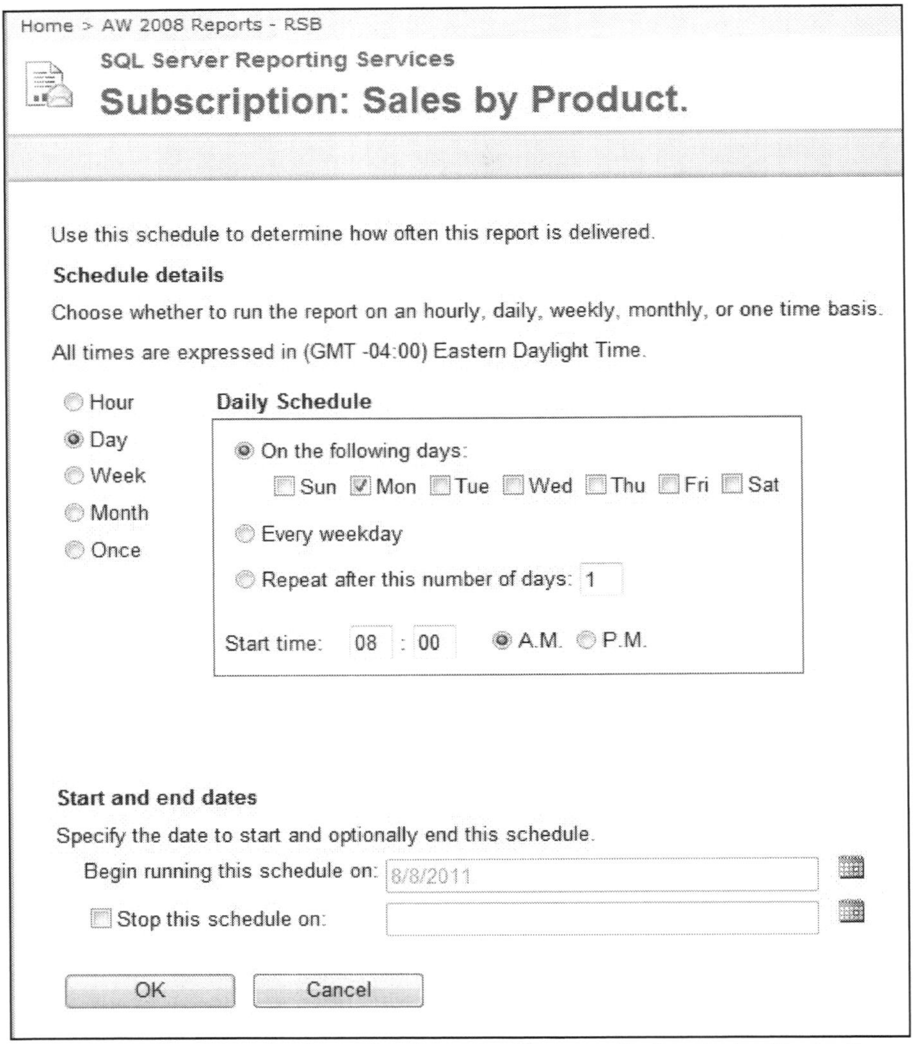

Home > AW 2008 Reports - RSB

SQL Server Reporting Services

Subscription: Sales by Product.

Use this schedule to determine how often this report is delivered.

Schedule details

Choose whether to run the report on an hourly, daily, weekly, monthly, or one time basis.

All times are expressed in (GMT -04:00) Eastern Daylight Time.

○ Hour

◉ Day

○ Week

○ Month

○ Once

Daily Schedule

◉ On the following days:

☐ Sun ☑ Mon ☐ Tue ☐ Wed ☐ Thu ☐ Fri ☐ Sat

○ Every weekday

○ Repeat after this number of days: 1

Start time: 08 : 00   ◉ A.M. ○ P.M.

Start and end dates

Specify the date to start and optionally end this schedule.

Begin running this schedule on: 8/8/2011

☐ Stop this schedule on:

OK   Cancel

Figure 2-15 Subscription Delivery Schedule Details

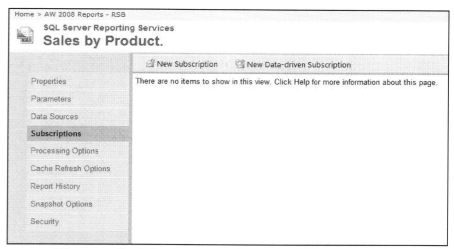

Figure 2-16 A Report's Subscription Page

The My Subscriptions navigation button in the Report Manager's toolbar in the upper right corner will display the My Subscriptions page shown in Figure 2-17. Here, all of your subscriptions will be listed, and from this page you can edit or delete them.

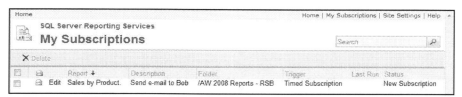

Figure 2-17 My Subscriptions Page

That's it for the tour of the Report Manager. Now on to the Report Builder.

Chapter 3 - Report Builder 3.0

As noted earlier Report Builder is a report authoring application that creates reports to be published on the Report Server. Report Builder 1.0 which was installed with SQL Server 2008 has been superseded by Report Builder 3.0 (RB3). RB3 may be installed separately from a msi file downloaded from the Microsoft Download Center. It requires the Microsoft .Net Framework version 3.5 to be installed on your computer.

RB3 offers a number of enhancements over version 1.0 including a Microsoft Office-optimized report authoring environment, a new Tablix data region that combines the table, matrix, and list formats from 1.0 version, and use of any data sources such as the SQL Server Database Engine, Analysis Services, Oracle, Microsoft Access, etc. instead of being limited to data sources and models in the Report Server. It now includes maps, Sparklines, Databars, and a Report Parts Gallery.

The following is only an introduction to RB3 and Reporting Services. There are a number of features that are slighted and some not even mentioned. Please see other sources such as RB3 Help, SQL Server Books Online, or books about Reporting Services for more complete coverage.

In RB3 you can use wizards to create tables, matrices, and map type reports or build reports from scratch. Most of report creation is done by dragging and dropping tools on a workspace, and you can add textboxes, images, gauges, subreports, and conditional formatting. You can modify data with filters, sort it, add drill-through reports, and add formulas and expressions. The reports can be saved to the report server or to your computer.

You start RB3 just like any other application by clicking on it in the Start menu prior to Windows 8, by double clicking on the exe file or a shortcut, or clicking on the Report Builder button in the Report Manager taskbar. Although it interacts with the Report Server, it is independent of it. Its appearance at start is shown in Figure 3-1. The Report Data panel is on the left, Properties on the right, the design surface (canvas) in the left center, the report part gallery in the right center, and groupings on the bottom. A Getting Started page is displayed on top where you may choose frequently used options. You may disable the Getting Started page by checking the box on the bottom.

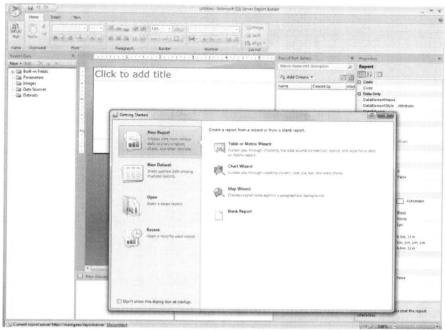

Figure 3-1 Report Builder 3.0 GUI

RB3 has an Office-type ribbon user interface at the top with three tabs: Home, Insert, and View. Partial screen shots of those ribbons and the Report Builder button are shown in Figure 3-2. In the figure the Home ribbon essentially offers formatting options and the Run button on it to run and view a report. The Insert menu lists objects that can be used in a report with the Table, Matrix, Chart, and Map objects having drop-down menus which offer two options: using a wizard or inserting the object directly, e.g., for the table object the option would be Table Wizard or Insert Table. There is not a separate toolbox panel as in some other applications like Visual Studio or BIDS. The View menu allows the selection of what appears on the interface surface: the data, properties, and groupings panels and the ruler. RB3 has a more simplified and streamlined GUI than the Report Designer in Visual Studio that we looked at in Chapter 2. The final image shows a drop-down menu similar to the File menu in Office applications. This is displayed by clicking on what I call the Report Builder button in the upper left corner of the window. There you can create new reports, open previous reports, save the current report, and display option menus.

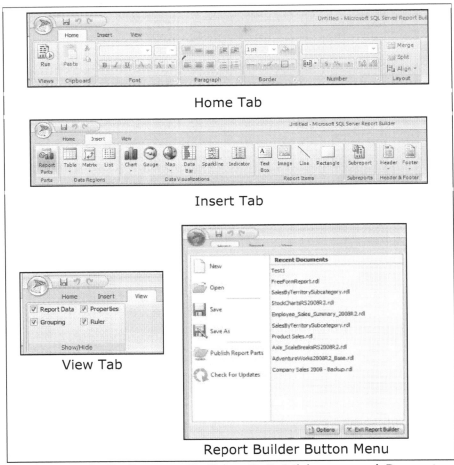

Figure 3-2 Report Builder 3.0 Ribbons and Report Button Menu

Now for three report fundamentals: data sources, query designers, and data regions.

Data Sources

Each report requires a data source. Data sources can be either shared or embedded. Shared data sources are stored on the Report Server and can be used in any reports given appropriate permissions. We discussed creating data sources in the Report Manager earlier in the previous chapter. Embedded data sources are local to the specific report. The connection information in an embedded report is contained only in that report and cannot be used for other reports. If an embedded data source is required in another report, the connection must be specified anew there as well. If a shared data source contains the data you need for a report, then use it. If a shared data source is not available, you have three options: use an embedded data source, go to the Report Manager and create a new shared data source, or ask the IT folks to create a shared data source using Reporting Services.

Data Sources with the Wizard

Regardless of whether you will use a shared or embedded data source or whether you will create your report with the wizard or manually, you will work with a data source or dataset properties dialog boxes like the one in Figure 3-3 for the Table wizard. If the data source that you need is not on the list, click on "Create a dataset" and then Next to display the Choose a connection to a data source window as in Figure 3-4. If the data source you want is not on the list, click the Browse button to view the shared data sources as in Figure 3-5. This file list is a view of the directory structure in the Report Manager shown previously in Figure 2-2. Click on any row in the list to view the contents of that folder. In this particular list only two folders contain shared data sources: Data Sources and Models. If you click on a folder that does not contain a data source, the resultant window will be empty.

Figure 3-3 Initial Dataset Dialog Box for the Wizard

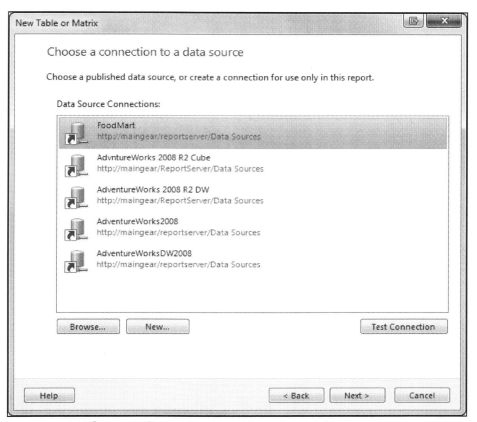

Figure 3-4 Connection Data Source

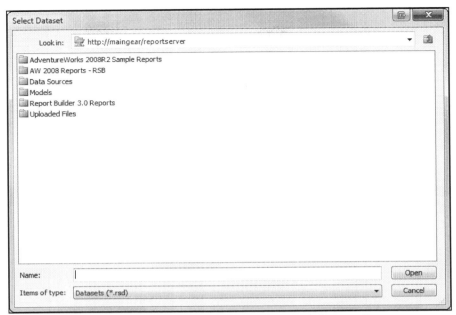

Figure 3-5 Browse for a Shared Data Source

If the data source that you need is not available as a shared data source and you cannot or choose not to create one or have one created for you, then you will have to use an embedded data source. In this case, click the "Create a dataset" button and the Next button in Figure 3-3 to bring up the Data Source Properties dialog box in Figure 3-6.

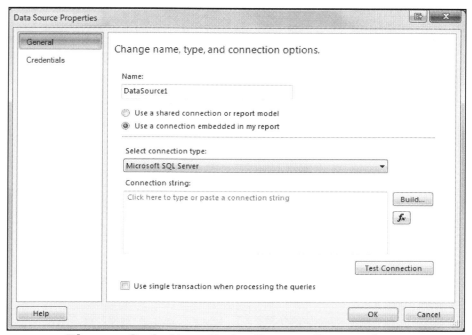

Figure 3-6 New Data Source Properties

To define a new embedded data source you give it a name (here DataSource1 is the default), select the embedded connection type, and build the connection string. Figure 3-7 shows the partial listbox for the connection type. I used the SQL Server connection type to create data sources from databases on my instance of SQL Server and the Analysis Services connection type to create a data source for the AdventureWorks Cube. There many other connection types available as you can see in the figure. If one is not specifically identified on the list, then you can probably find what you need in the OLE DB connection type or define a connection via an ODBC connection string. For example, you could connect to an Access 2010 database by using the OLE DB connection type with the Microsoft Office 12.0 Access Database Engine OLE DB Provider. A database connection to the Northwind Access database is shown in Figure 3-8.

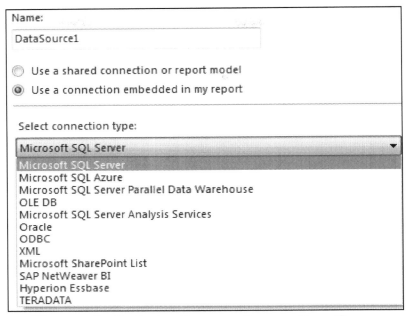

Figure 3-7 Data Source Connection Types

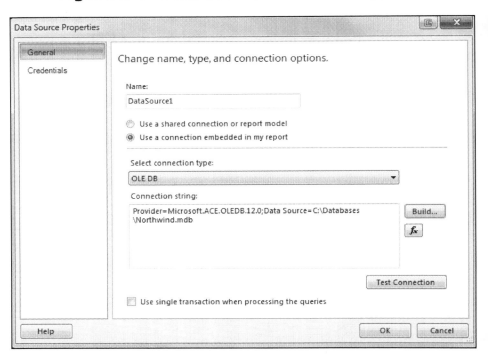

Figure 3-8 Access 2010 Data Source Connection

Since you will likely use SQL Server databases as data sources, let's look at how to build a connection to them. If you select Microsoft SQL Server as the connection type as in Figure 3-6 and then click the Build button, a Connection Properties dialog box is displayed as in Figure 3-9. You have the option of changing the data source type by clicking the Change button, and you select the server instance by entering its name in the Server Name textbox or selecting a server that is shown on a list when you click on the down arrowhead. In Figure 3-10 I entered my server's name, MAINGEAR. At this point you may test the connection by clicking the Text Connection button at the bottom. If the test succeeds, then you may select the database for the connection from the drop-down list. In Figure 3-10 I selected the old FoodMart database. Clicking the OK button at the bottom will take you back to the Data Source Properties dialog box (Figure 3-6) with the appropriate connection showing in the Connection String textbox, and clicking OK will take back to the to the next wizard page.

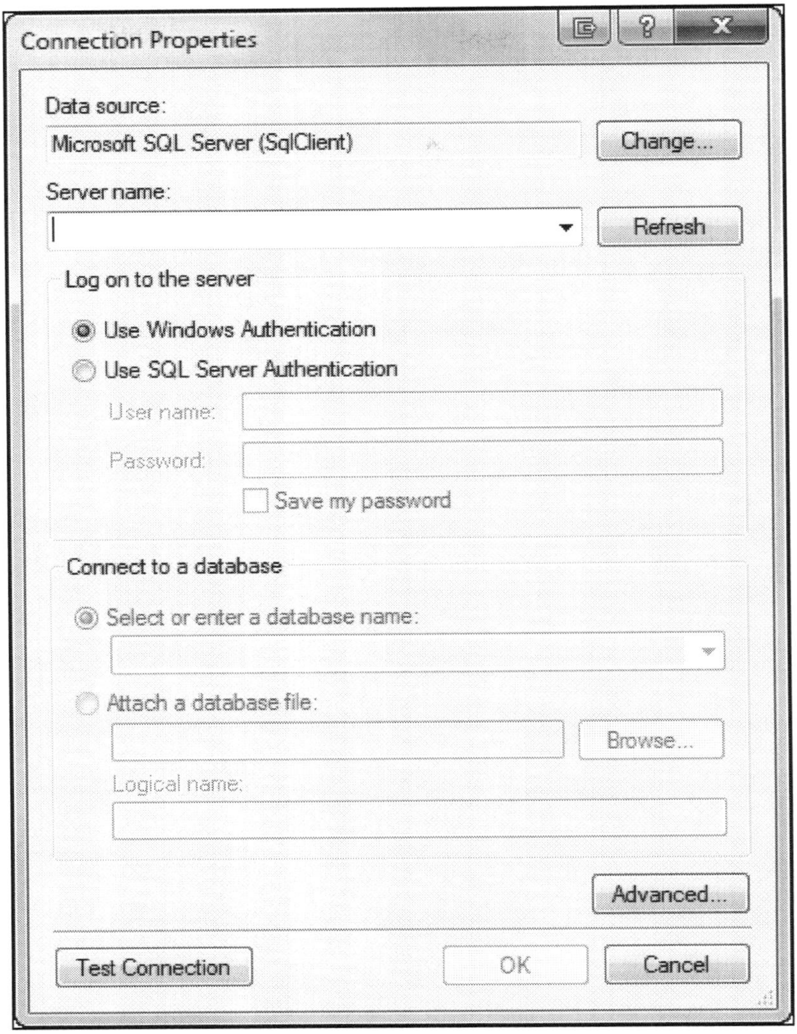

Figure 3-9 New Connection Dialog Box

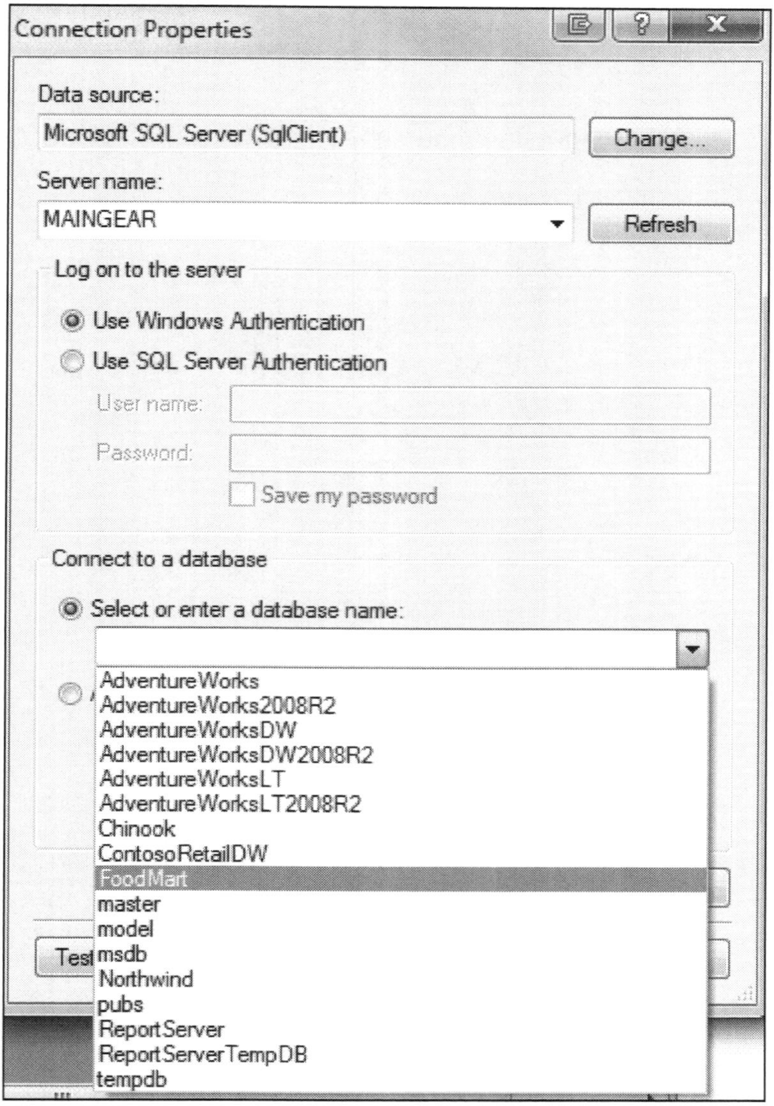

Figure 3-10 Connection to a SQL Server Database

Manual Data Source Connections

Starting with the initial RB3 window in Figure 3-1 we may create a new data source manually by clicking on New in the Report Data panel on the left which presents the drop-down listbox in Figure 3-11. Clicking on Data Source there brings up a Data Source

Properties dialog box as in Figure 3-5. You may also right click on the Data Sources Folder to display that box. Selecting the shared connection option keeps you in this view where you may either select a shared connection used previously from the list or browse for other available shared connections by clicking on the Browse button which will bring up the Select Data source window shown in Figure 3-3. Selecting the embedded connection option will bring up a window similar to the one in Figure 3-4. Proceed to create the connection and return to the RB3 main window where a new data source has been added in the Report Data panel as in Figure 3-12. Double clicking on the new data source, DataSource1, will take you back to the dialog box in Figure 3-8.

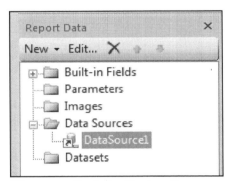

Figure 3-11 Report Data New List

Figure 3-12 Data Source Added

The next step in manually creating a data source is to construct a dataset to be used in the report from the data source. When using the query designer with the wizard as discussed below, a dataset will be automatically be created. We'll cover constructing a dataset for a manually created data source later in the description of query designers.

Query Designers

Each report uses a query to specify data, the columns and rows that will be used in it. The query designer is an easy to use, drag and drop GUI that creates the query statement in the appropriate query language, e.g., SQL for relational databases, MDX for cubes, etc., unless only a text-based designer is supported. The presentation of the designer user interface varies depending on the type of data source: an Analysis Services cube, a relational database, a report model, and a few others. We will explore the Designer for an Analysis Services database.

The Query Designer shown in Figure 3-13 uses the AdventureWorks Cube as a shared data source. You may change the Analysis Services data source by clicking on the Cube Selection button, the one with the dots, to the right of the current cube name (AdventureWorks). Note that you are limited to changing to an available data source of the same type, in this case, another cube. There are four main areas on the Designer surface: Metadata contains the list of data available – for our example measures, KPIs, and dimensions since we're using a cube; Calculated Members local to the report (there are none yet in this initial setup); the Design and Query View panel on the lower right; and the Filter panel above it.

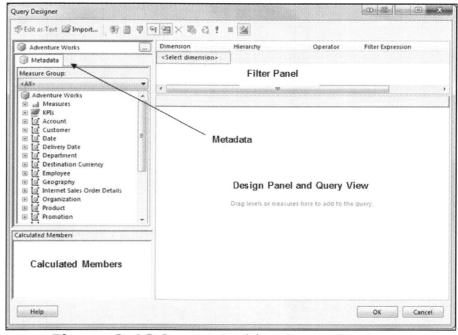

Figure 3-13 Report Builder Query Designer

Fields and values are added to a query by selecting an object in the Metadata panel, and then dragging and dropping it onto the Design panel. Items selected and dropped will insert all items included beneath it into the query, e.g., if I dropped the Measures item into the designer, all of the measures in the cube would be inserted into the query.

As an example of building a query, I expanded Measures to get to the list of measures in Figure 3-14a, and then the Internet Sales folder for the list of individual Internet sales measures in Figure 3-14b. I then dragged and dropped the Internet Gross Profit Margin and Internet Sales Amount fields onto the design surface. I also dropped the Category and Subcategory attributes from the Products dimension and the Calendar Quarter from the Date dimension as shown in Figure 3-15. Last, I dropped Calendar year from the Date dimension into the Filter panel. This essentially completes the query.

 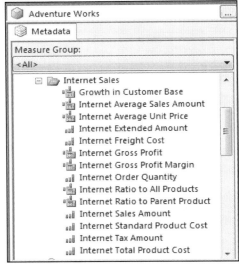

Table 3-14a Measures Expanded   **Table 3-14b** Internet Sales Expanded

Figure 3-14 Query Fields Selection

By including the Calendar Year in the Filter panel the report based on the query will have its records limited (filtered) to the value(s) specified by the filter. If you click on the Date.Calendar Year box in the Hierarchy column, a drop-down list box allows you to change the filter attribute as shown in Figure 3-16a. Similarly, clicking on the box below the Operator heading brings up the operator-type listbox as in Figure 3-16b. The time period to display in this particular report is selected in the drop-down listbox accessed under the Filter Expression column heading as in Figure 3-16c.

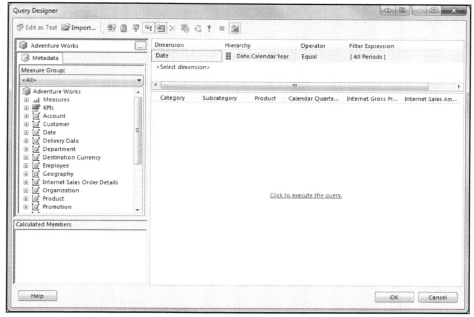

Figure 3-15 The Completed Query

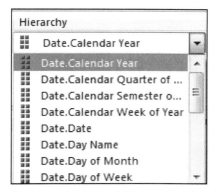

Figure 3-16a Hierarchy List

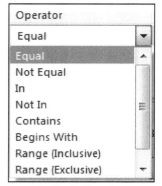

Figure 3-16b Operator List

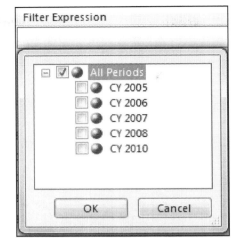

Figure 3-16c Filter Expression List

Figure 3-16 Filter Configuration Lists

If you prefer to have the filter act as a parameter in the report, i.e., an attribute whose value the user can specify when the report is viewed as shown in Figure 3-17 (All Periods are selected there), then click on the Parameter checkbox which is shown by moving the horizontal scroll bar at the bottom of the Filter panel all the way to the right. With the parameter enabled the Filter Expression becomes the default presentation in the reports initial rendering. By including the Calendar Year in the Filter panel as a parameter the report based on the query will have the capability to display the data by the calendar year(s) selected by the user.

Dimension	Hierarchy	Operator	Filter Expression	Param...
Date	Date.Calendar Year	Equal	{ All Periods }	☑
<Select dimension>				

Category	Subcategory	Product	Calendar Quarter ...	Internet Gross Profit	Internet Sales Amo...	
Accessories	Bike Racks	Hitch Rack - 4-Bike	CY Q1	5558.88	8880	
Accessories	Bike Racks	Hitch Rack - 4-Bike	CY Q2	7286.64	11640	
Accessories	Bike Racks	Hitch Rack - 4-Bike	CY Q3	6535.44	10440	
Accessories	Bike Racks	Hitch Rack - 4-Bike	CY Q4	5258.4	8400	
Accessories	Bike Stands	All-Purpose Bike S...	CY Q1	5175.768	8268	
Accessories	Bike Stands	All-Purpose Bike S...	CY Q2	6668.778	10653	

Figure 3-17 Filter Parameter Checkbox

To remove a field from the design surface just click on its name (the column heading) and drag it away from the panel. To execute the query, if it has not run already, click on the red exclamation point (!) button or the "Click to execute the query" message in the design panel. The results are displayed in Query View at the bottom of Figure 3-17. It's important to run the query at this point in case that there are execution errors.

The buttons at the top of the query designer appear above Table 3-1 which describes their function. Search for "Analysis Services MDX Query Designer User Interface" in RB3 Help for more information. Clicking on the last icon button in the list, the Design-Query mode toggle shows the query code in what was the Filter panel, in this case in MDX query language, as in Figure 3-18. Clicking again will return to design mode.

1	**2**	**3**	**4**	**5**	**6**	**7**	**8**	**9**	**10**

Button	Description
1	Refresh metadata.
2	Add calculated member.
3	Show empty cells.
4	Auto execute.
5	Show aggregations.
6	Query parameters.
7	Prepare query.
8	Execute query (Run).
9	Cancel Query.
10	Design mode.

Table 3-1 Query Designer Buttons

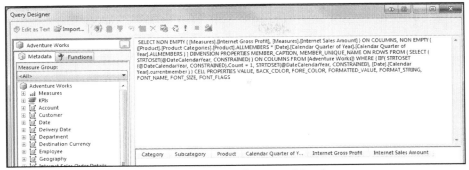

Figure 3-18 Query Mode

Calculated Members

Calculated members are dimensions or measures that do not exist in the data source but are calculated from those that are. You use a calculated member in the same manner as those that already exist in the cube.

You create a new calculated member by either clicking on the Calculated Member Builder icon button in the toolbar or right clicking on the Calculated Members panel. Either way you get to the Calculated Member Builder shown in Figure 3-19. First, give the new calculated member a name and select the Parent Hierarchy, the place in the Metadata list where the new calculated member will appear. I'll keep calculated members in Measures. Note that Parent Member is disabled if the Parent Hierarchy is Measures. Next, create the MDX expression by dragging and dropping Metadata and/or functions into the Expression textbox or by writing MDX code directly (Ugh!).

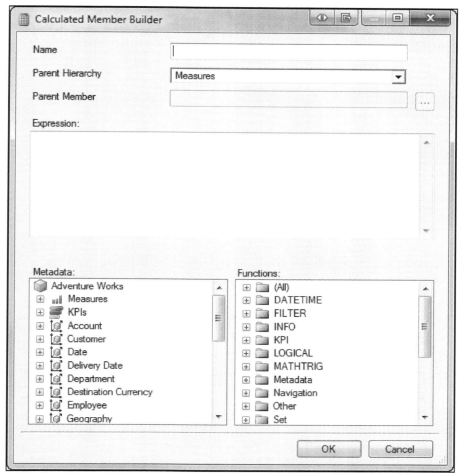

Figure 3-19 Calculated Member Builder

In Figure 3-20 I created a very simple calculated measure to compute the sales tax rate by dragging and dropping the Internet Tax Amount and the Internet Sales Amount from the Metadata panel in the Measures folder into the Expression textbox. I added the divide operator (/) and multiplied the result by 100 to compute a percentage. Click OK to return to the Query designer where the new calculated member will appear in the Calculated Members panel ready to use. Neat! Note that the calculated members created with Visual Studio/BIDS in Analysis Services are still available and are listed in the Metadata. In fact we used one, Internet Gross Profit Margin, in building the example query above.

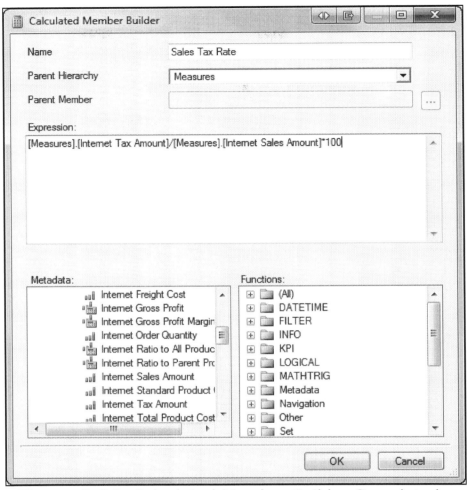

Figure 3-20 Calculated Member Builder Completed

Clicking OK will get you back to the query designer. Clicking OK in the query designer window will complete the query design and take you either further on in the report wizard or back to the RB3 main window depending upon where you started the query design process. When you return to the query designer main window you will find a new entry in the Report Data panel on the left of the RB3 main window in the background as shown in Figure 3-21. In this figure the entry "AdventureWorksCube" is the data source name, and the data fields to be used are listed under the dataset, InternetSales.

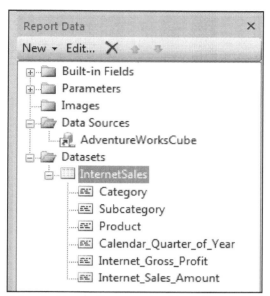

Figure 3-21 A New Query in the Report Data Panel

Manual Dataset Construction

Earlier we described how to create a data source manually as shown in Figure 3-11. Continuing with that here, a dataset is required to use data from the data source in a report. A dataset lists the fields and attributes that will be available to the report and is specified in a query as exemplified by the list under InternetSales in Figure 3-21 above. You may create more than one dataset for a data source. To create a new dataset either click on New or right click on the data source in the Report Data panel and select Add Dataset. Either method will bring up the Dataset Properties dialog box shown in Figure 3-22. You may rename the dataset from its default name and select or create a new data source if the one showing is not correct. Clicking on the Query Designer button will take you to the query designer as in Figure 3-13. Clicking the Import button will take you to a file explorer where you can select items that already have datasets defined, e.g., report files (files with a rdl file extension), reports in the Report Manager, etc. Figure 3-23 shows the Dataset Properties window after I imported a dataset from another report.

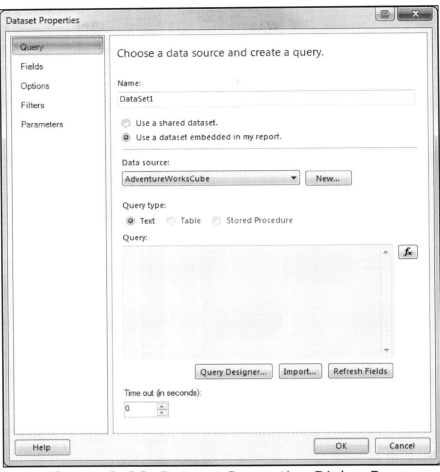

Figure 3-22 Dataset Properties Dialog Box

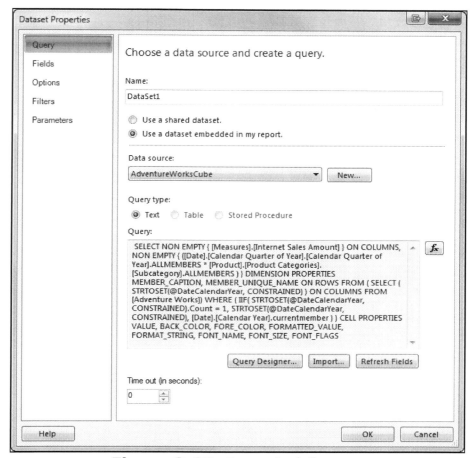

Figure 3-23 Imported Query

After the query is specified you may configure the dataset by using one or more of the items in the list in the panel on left side: Parameters lists the existing parameters, allows deleting existing ones, and adding new ones; Fields allows you to add or delete fields from the query; Options allows you to change collation, case sensitivity, and other options; And Filters allows you to add and delete filters. Since these actions are fairly straight forward, we'll not examine them in detail here. Clicking OK in the Query view returns you to the RB3 main page with the new dataset listed in the Report Data panel as shown in Figure 3-24.

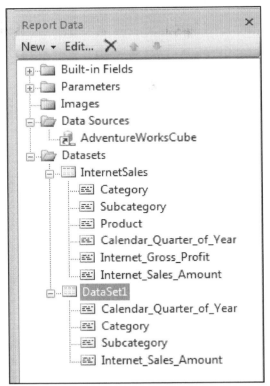

Figure 3-24 Completed New Dataset

Shared Datasets

You may store dataset configurations for reuse instead of having to recreate a dataset for each new report that uses it. To do that in RB3 select New Dataset from the Getting Started page or from the New Report or Dataset window which will display a data source list as in Figure 3-5 from which you specify the data source for the data set. After doing that, you will proceed to the Report Builder Query Designer (Figure 3-13) and proceed to build the query. Back in the Report Builder main page you would then save the dataset as a .rdl file to a folder in the Report Server or elsewhere. I save mine in a folder called Data Sets.

Data Regions

Data regions are used to display data in a report. There are three

types of data regions in RB3: tables, matrixes, and lists. We will
see how to use these data regions a bit later in this chapter. There
can be more than one data region in a report, and data regions
can be nested within other data regions.

Tables, matrixes, and lists are variations of the Tablix data region
which presents data in tabular form with rows and columns. The
default cell in a Tablix is a textbox but you can insert other report
objects such as an image.

A Tablix without groupings presents data in detail as defined by
the underlying query. However, data may be aggregated in a
Tablix by using groups for, say, drilling-down. Figure 3-25 shows
the grouping panes at the bottom of the designer window. Groups
are organized as a hierarchy in a tree-like structure. For example,
row groups for products may have product category at the top of
the hierarchy (the parent), product subcategory below and
subordinate to the product category (its child), and then the
product itself at the bottom of the hierarchy as the child of the
product subcategory. Similarly, column groups could have
calendar year as the parent with calendar quarter as its child.
We'll see later how groups can be used to create interactive
reports with drill-down capabilities. There's considerably more to
learn about the Tablix data region than we can present here.
Please see Report Builder 3.0 Help for advanced topics.

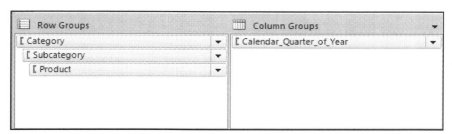

Figure 3-25 Tablix Groping Example

So far in this description of RB3 we have learned how to create
data sources, data sets, and data regions but we have yet to build
a report. There are two ways to do that: with a wizard or
manually. We will examine both.

Using the Report Builder Wizard

The obvious way to start building a report is to click on one of the two option presented on the design surface of a new report as in Figure 3-1: Table or Matrix or Chart. The other way is to click on Table, Matrix, or Chart on the Insert Ribbon and select the wizard drop-down option. Either way will bring up the data source connection dialog box as in Figure 3-3 which leads to the Query Designer that we learned about above. When the query design is complete, click OK to move on to the next window to arrange the fields in the Tablix. Using the query that we created above the Arrange Fields window initially appears as in Figure 3-26 with the fields that we included in the query listed in the Available Fields panel. We can drag and drop these fields into positions for a table (just columns of data if you remember) or rows and columns for a matrix style report. The Values panel will contain the measures that will be the table's or matrix's cell values.

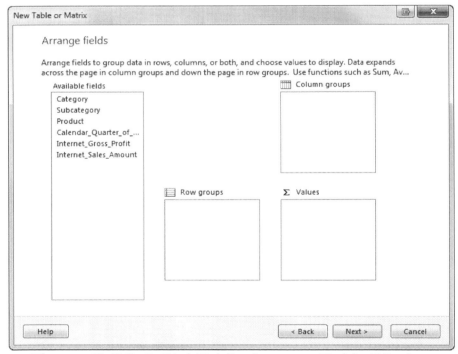

Figure 3-26 Initial Tablix Arrange Fields Window

In Figure 3-27 I dragged Calendar_Quarter_of_Year into the

Column groups for the column heading, Category and Subcategory into Row groups for row headings, and Internet_Sales_Amount into Σ Values (Sum of Values) for cell values. I left the Internet_Gross_Margin calculated measure alone for now. Note that the row and column groups will appear in the report designer groupings panel per our discussion of Figure 3-25.

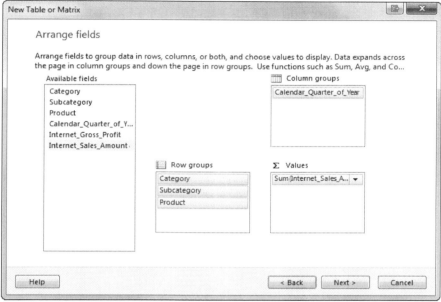

Figure 3-27 Completed Tablix Arrange Fields Window

You select the layout style in the next window shown in Figure 3-28. If you want subtotals and grand totals in the report, leave that box checked. Note that the Expand/collapse groups box it checked. This allows drill-down in the report. You can also set this toggle later by tinkering with the properties of groups in the Groupings panel.

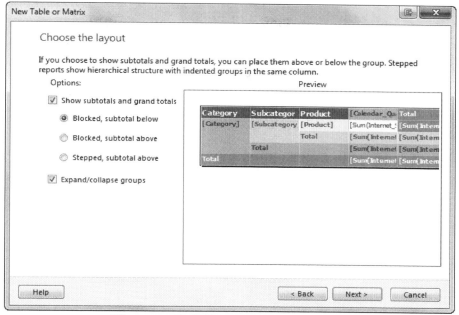

Figure 3-28 Layout Window

The next window in Figure 3-29 allows you to choose a report style. Just click on a style name to view a preview. Here the Ocean style is previewed.

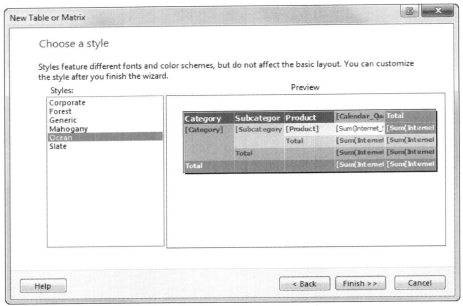

Figure 3-29 Style Window

When you click on Finish, you will return to the RB3 main page as in Figure 3-30 which now shows the report in design view on the design surface. You may now preview it by clicking on Run in the upper left corner of the window. If you did that, you would see the mess in Figure 3-31. (Note that the Report Server must be accessible to preview a report.) It's obvious that the report needs a lot more work to make it presentable.

The Run tab in Figure 3-31, the only tab on the Ribbon in preview view, contains actions and menus related to the report such as zooming, printing, and exporting. The Parameters button in the Options menu hides or unhides the parameters bar below the Ribbon if parameters are included in the report design. Note that with parameters visible, clicking on the button in the Parameters bar displays the drop-down listbox to select, in this case, the years to include in the report as we saw back in Figure 3-16. To return to design view just click on Design in the upper left corner.

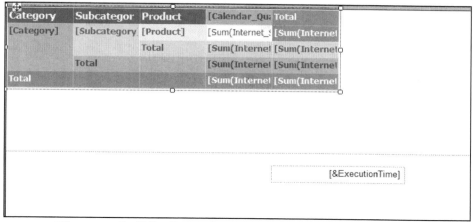

Figure 3-30 Initial Report in Design View

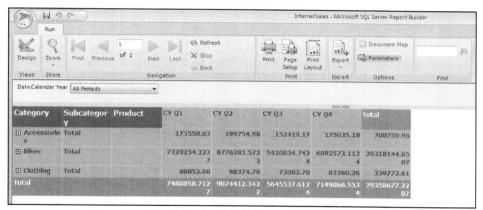

Figure 3-31 Initial Report Preview

A report can be saved as regular file in the usual way. I saved this report as "InternetSales.rdl" in a directory on my local hard drive. However, if you want the report to be available on the Report Manager, say so other users can view it, you may save it to the Report Server as well. To do that select Save As to bring up the Save As Dialog box and click Recent Sites and Servers which, in this case, lists the folders on my report server as in Figure 3-32. I saved the report in the Report Builder 3 Reports folder by clicking on that folder and then on Save. You can see in Figure 3-33 that the report was published to the Report Manager. We'll expand on saving reports at the end of the chapter.

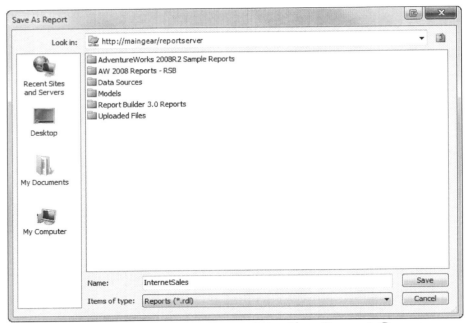

Figure 3-32 Save a Report to the Report Server

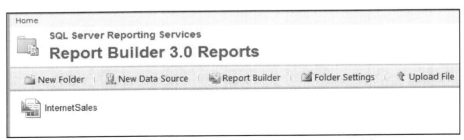

Figure 3-33 Report Available in Report Manager

Designing a Report Manually

When you open RB3 or click on New from the Office-type button in the upper left corner you will be presented with the report designer as shown in Figure 3-1. Let's start out with a clean design surface as in Figure 3-34 by deleting all the items that RB3 creates when you begin. You do this by clicking on an object to select it (when selected a frame will appear around it) and then delete it. You may remove the footer by clicking on Footer on the Insert tab and selecting Remove Footer. Ok, now we have an empty surface. To resize the canvas just drag a border to the desired shape. By the way, we're using the report rdl file in which we created a data source and dataset back in Figure 3-24.

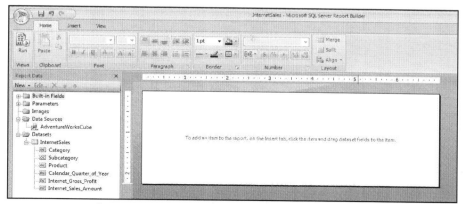

Figure 3-34 Clean Design Surface

For the example let's insert a matrix-type table into the report by clicking on Matrix on the Insert tab and selecting Insert Matrix. Then, move the mouse pointer to the design surface and draw a rectangle for the matrix. If there was no dataset defined, RB3 would bring up the Dataset Properties dialog box as in Figure 3-22. However, since a dataset exists already, it will create an empty matrix-type framework on the design surface as shown in Figure 3-35a. To change the design of the matrix click anywhere within it and boarders will appear on its perimeter. Then right clicking on an element within will display an options window. In the case of Figure 3-35b I clicked on a column heading to display column options. I would then select Insert Columns and Inside Group Right to insert another column. Columns can be resized by dragging on their boarders.

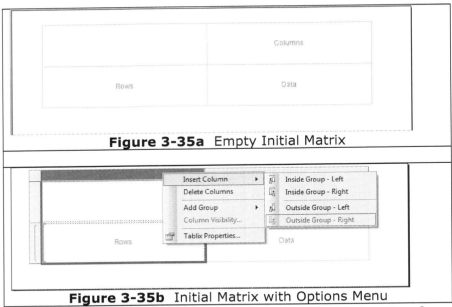

Figure 3-35a Empty Initial Matrix

Figure 3-35b Initial Matrix with Options Menu

Figure 3-35 Matrix Framework on the Design Surface

Going back to Figure 3-35a now all that remains to complete definition of the report is to drag and drop objects from the Report Data pane onto the framework as shown in Figure 3-36.

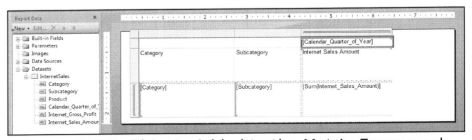

Figure 3-36 Objects Added to the Matrix Framework

This is essentially the same report that we built with the wizard above with calendar year as the row heading, product category and subcategory as column headings, and sales amount as the cell values. The dimensions were automatically added to the groupings panel at the bottom (not shown). Instead of dragging and dropping row and column to the cells in the framework, we could have dragged and dropped them into the grouping panel to achieve the same result. Figure 3-37 shows the preview of the report and how really basic the design is at this point. Notice that it does have the calendar year parameter that we specified in the query design.

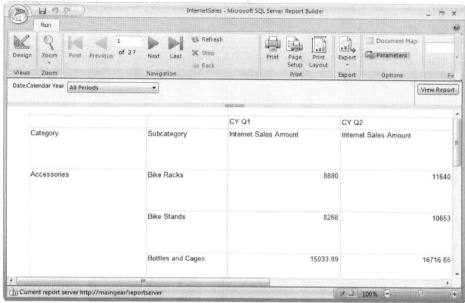

Figure 3-37 New Report Preview

Tuning the Report

Both reports we have created so far, the ones in Figures 3-31 and 3-37, are not presentation quality to say the least. This is expected as all reports require tinkering to get into presentable form. Their initial construction is only a place to start the design process, and when the basic structure is there we can proceed to enhance and polish the layout. In the description below I'll try to cover the major design options including adding other objects to the report such as subreports, charts, and images; formatting the report; and adding drill-down and drill-through capabilities. There are other options that we will not examine but knowledge about the basic ones should allow you to proceed on your own with the others.

Basic Report Structure and Properties

The basic report structure is shown in the partial screen shot of an empty report (except for the three textboxes used to identify the sections) on RB3's design surface (canvas) in Figure 3-38. The Page Header will be displayed on the top of all pages, and the page footer at the bottom of all pages. Headers and footers can contain a variety of objects such as textboxes, images, shapes, and so on. The Body can contain any type of report object such as tables, charts, images, textboxes, etc. Note that the Body textbox has a frame around it which means that object is currently selected, and the four arrow icon there represents a point to click and drag to reposition the object on the surface. You can change the shape of the object by dragging the double arrows that appear when the mouse pointer is positioned over the small squares on the perimeter. Headers and footers can be inserted and removed via the Header & Footer menu on the Insert tab. Header, footer, and body areas can be resized using the double arrow to drag the boundary line.

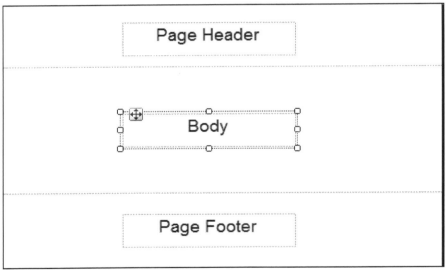

Figure 3-38 New Basic Report Design Surface

The size of the design surface canvas can be resized by moving the mouse over the perimeter boundary of the canvas until a double arrow appears, then clicking and holding the double arrow while dragging it to change the shape. Right clicking on the designer panel outside of the canvas displays the Report

Properties dialog box as in Figure 3-39 where you can set various properties in the Page Setup view.

Report Properties Code view presents an area to insert custom Visual Basic code into the report. (It appears to me that this is Visual Basic .Net and not Visual Basic for Applications code.) A few examples of custom code are listed below:

```
Public Const MyName = "Bob Bussom"
Public Dim NumberOfCopies as Integer =1
Public RecipientEmail as String =
"someone@somewhere.com"

Public Function ChangeWord(ByVal s As String) As String
Dim strBuilder As New System.Text.StringBuilder(s)
If s.Contains("Bike") Then
strBuilder.Replace("Bike", "Bicycle")
Return strBuilder.ToString()
Else : Return s
End If
End Function
```

The first line defines a constant; the second an integer variable, and the third a string variable. The frivolous function copied from Report Builder 3.0 Help replaces the word Bike with Bicycle if the string passed to it contains the word Bike. Constants, variables and other custom code may be used in expressions which will be addressed later in this chapter.

The Reference view provides for setting references to assemblies and classes, specifically dll files if you know what they are. (References is an advanced topic so we'll pass by it here.) The Variables view allows adding other custom variables to a report.

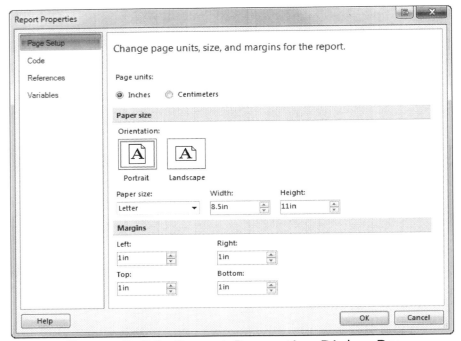

Figure 3-39 Report Properties Dialog Box

Back on the canvas right clicking on the header area and selecting Header Properties brings up the Page Header Properties dialog box as in Figure 3-40 where you can configure the header page, change the background fill color or insert a background image in the Fill view, and add a boarder in Border view. The same properties are available in the Page Footer Properties and Body Properties dialog boxes.

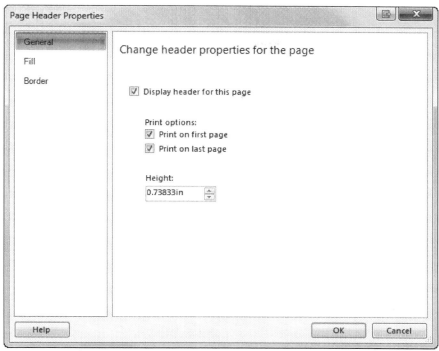

Figure 3-40 Page Header Dialog Box

Formatting a Tablix

Let's return to the report presented in Figure 3-30 and in preview view in Figure 3-31 where the formatting of the table needs some adjustments: (1) the numbers in cells and in the totals row and column should be in an acceptable format; (2) the headings in the top row should be centered; (3) the Category and Subcategory columns should be widened to avoid text wrapping; and (4) the fonts may need changing. But before we get to that notice that when the Tablix was created with the wizard a title textbox and a footer with an execution datatime value were automatically added. We could remove them but we'll leave them for now.

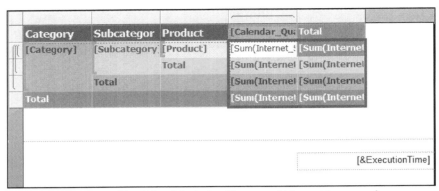

Figure 3-41 Matrix Formatting Example

1. To reformat the numbers, select all of the cells that display numbers as shown in Figure 3-41 (the dark border shows the selected area). You then have two options: use the Number menu on the Home Ribbon directly or the Text Box Properties dialog box. We'll look at both options.

Number Menu: I want to format the numbers in a format with commas as the thousands separators but with no decimal places. So I selected number from the drop-down listbox in the Number menu that is currently set to default and then selected Number, clicked the comma box to activate separators, and then removed all decimal places by repeat clicking on the .00→0 box.

Text Box Properties: Click on the tiny arrow at the bottom of the Number menu there to bring up the Text Box Properties Dialog Box as shown in Figure 3-42. There you can change the name of the box, value, and sizing options; format a number or date; change alignment; change the font; insert borders and fill; change when the report is visible; enable sorting, and specify an action (we will get into actions a bit later). So, I selected Number and checked Use 1000 separator to change the number format this way.

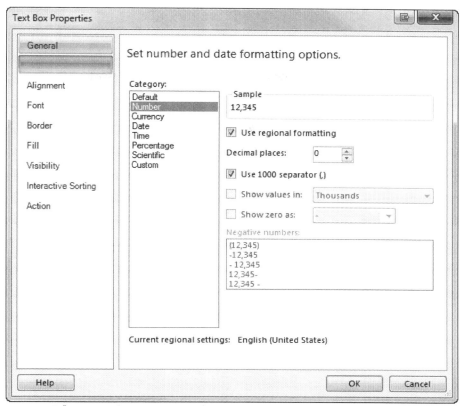

Figure 3-42 Textbox Properties Dialog Box

2. Centered Headings: Select the entire report heading row, and then click the center alignment icon just above the Paragraph title on the Home tab.

3. Column Width: As you can see in Figure 3-30 the Category and Subcategory columns need to be widened to avoid word wrap. So, I just dragged the right boundary in the gray area at the top of each of the column to widen them.

4. Font: Select the entire table, and then select the font characteristics from the Font menu on the Home Ribbon that you prefer. I selected the Verdana font and left all else as is for now.

I also took the liberty of adding a title to the report in the "Click to add title" textbox that was inserted by the wizard by just typing in the box. Regardless of the approach the report now looks like that in Figure 3-43. It's much better, but it still need some work.

Category	Subcategory	Product	CY Q1	CY Q2	CY Q3	CY Q4	Total
Date.Calendar Year	All Periods						
Internet Sales by Product							
⊟ Accessories	⊟ Bike Racks	Hitch Rack – 4-Bike	8,880	11,640	10,440	8,400	39360
		Total	8880	11640	10440	8400	39360
	⊞ Bike Stands	Total	9268	10653	8745	11925	39591
	⊞ Bottles and Cages	Total	15034	16717	11077	13970	56798
	⊞ Cleaners	Total	1781	2043	1590	1805	7219
	⊞ Fenders	Total	11583	13276	10001	11759	46620
	⊞ Helmets	Total	55634	67706	46187	55809	225336
	⊞ Hydration Packs	Total	10888	11163	8578	9678	40308
	⊞ Tires and Tubes	Total	61482	66558	55601	61688	245529
	Total		173551	199755	152419	175035	700760
⊞ Bikes	Total		7229254	8776283	5420035	6892573	28318145
⊞ Clothing	Total		86054	98375	73084	82260	339773
Total			7488859	9074412	5645538	7149869	29358677

Figure 3-43 Reformatted Report

Adding a Chart

The Insert tab Ribbon in Figure 3-2 shows all of the items that can be added to a report. We have already seen how to add a table or matrix in a report so we won't repeat that here. To add a chart just click on Chart and select either Chart Wizard or Insert Chart from the drop-down list. If you go the Chart Wizard route, you will be lead through a series of windows starting with one to choose the dataset for the chart. If you choose to create a new dataset, you will proceed to a data source connections dialog box similar to the one in Figure 3-3. You would proceed on from there as usual. If you select an existing dataset, e.g., InternetSales in our example, then the Chart Type dialog box will appear as in Figure 3-44 where you select the chart type. You then move on to arrange the chart fields as in Figure 3-45. Note that the Categories list is displayed on the horizontal axis, the Values list on the vertical axis, and the series list creates series. (A series is a separate variable to plot. For example. in a line chart with multiple lines each line on the chart is a separate series.). Next you would select the chart style and then finish it. I selected a column chart.

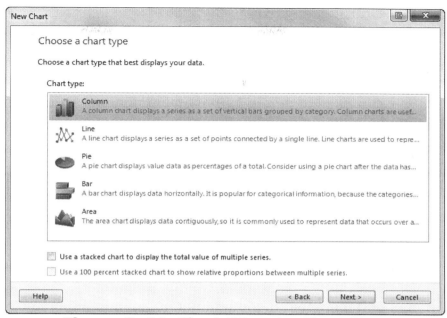

Figure 3-44 Chart Wizard - Chart Type

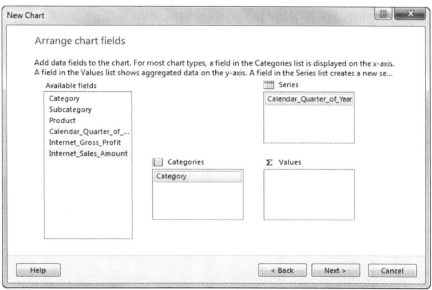

Figure 3-45 Chart Wizard - Chart Fields

When you return to the RB3 main page the new chart may be superimposed on some of the existing objects on the canvass. If so, just select the chart and move it to an appropriate place as I did in Figure 3-46. The image of the chart on the canvas in design view is only a stylized representation of it - the chart must be previewed to actually see it.

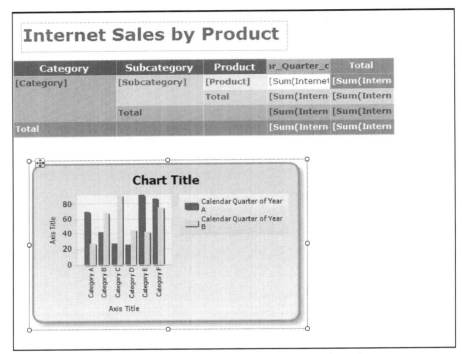

Figure 3-46 Example Chart on the Canvas

Figure 3-47 shows the report preview with the new chart. Notice that the bikes columns are far higher than those of accessories and clothing as you would expect by looking at the data in the table; the quarters of the year show up as series; the chart and axes need titles; and the vertical axis values need formatting. To change the title of an axis either double click it and enter the new title or go to the Axis Title Dialog Box by right clicking on the axis title. I used the former approach here. To reformat an axis either click on the axis and use the formatting controls on the Home tab or right click the axis to bring up the Axis Properties dialog box. I used the former approach to change the font on the horizontal axis categories to Verdana bold and the latter approach to reformat the vertical axis values.

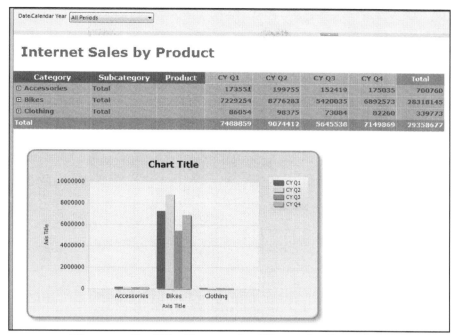

Figure 3-47 Example Chart in Preview

The Axis Properties dialog box for the vertical axis (called the Value axis by RB3) is shown in Figure 3-48. Properties can be changed there for axis options, labels, the font, number, tick marks, and the axis line. I used the Number view (see Figure 3-42) to set the number format to render sales in $000. I also inserted a chart title and changed to a bold font for the legend. The result is shown in preview view in Figure 3-49.

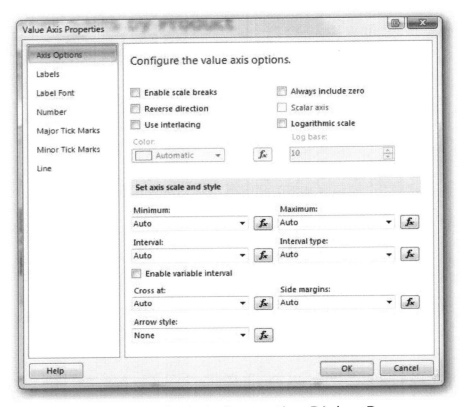

Figure 3-48 Axis Properties Dialog Box

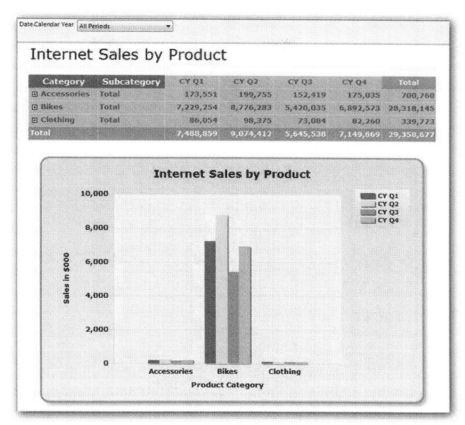

Figure 3-49 Reformatted Chart

The principle to learn here is that you can view and change the properties of any object in the chart by either clicking on it or using the Home tab controls or by right clicking on it to bring up a menu or dialog box. Indeed, these are basically the same approaches used in Microsoft Office applications, particularly Excel. For example, if you right click anywhere on the chart background, the menu in Figure 3-50 pops up. In that menu you can change the chart type, change various properties, and so on.

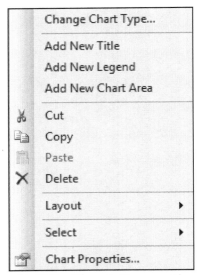

Figure 3-50 Chart Properties Menu

Adding a Gauge

Let's return to the report in Figure 3-30 and add a gauge. On the Insert tab you can either click on the Gauge icon and then draw a gauge on the canvas or double click on the Gauge icon. In either case the Select Gauge Type dialog box appears where, of course, you select the style of gauge that you want. There are twelve radial gauge templates all with some kind of dial and nine linear templates with thermometer or ruler images available. You use gauges to display data values.

Report Builder 3.0 Help identifies the gauge parts in the image below, and goes on to say that gauge forms cannot be interchanged as in Office application. Rather, the current gauge must be replaced with a new gauge. A gauge must have at least one scale, and other scales can be added.

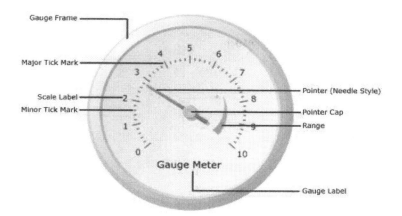

Gauges seem to be more difficult to work with than tables and charts, at least for me. Possibly this is because gauges only display one value on a scale. So, for example using a gauge to represent Internet Sales in our ongoing example in itself would be meaningless unless we added some maximum value so that the gauge would show the position of sales relative to that value. Additionally, a gauge displays aggregate sums or counts of a field, and, even if a group is included, the gauge only displays the value for the last member of the group. See Report Builder 3.0 Help or SQL Server Books Online for more info about this.

As an example I picked a simple radial gauge and selected Internet Gross Profit Margin as the metric to use because it has an absolute maximum value of 1.0 (100%). To add a data field to a gauge either drag the field from the Report Data pane to the drop zone that appears on the gauge image; display the drop zone by double clicking on the gauge image and then click on the tiny rectangular icon to show the list of available data fields; or right click on the gauge pointer and select pointer properties. I just dropped the Internet Gross Profit Margin field from the Report Data pane into the data drop zone. Figure 3-51 shows the drop zone with the gross margin field added to it in the lowest row in the drop-down table. Note that the field is initially set to the Sum of Internet Gross Profit Margin. I changed it to Avg (for Average) by clicking on the Internet Gross Profit row in the menu, clicking on Aggregate, and selecting Avg from the list. The figure also shows the menu list that appears when you right click the scale on the gauge.

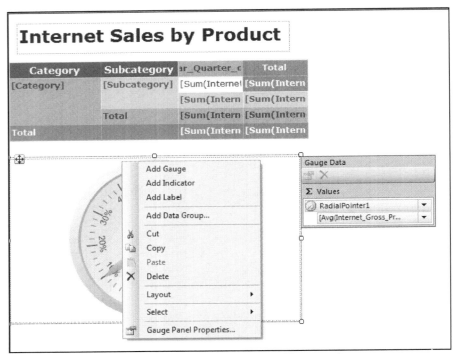

Figure 3-51 Gauge Example

To format the gauge scale click on scale properties to display the Scale Properties dialog box as in Figure 3-52 where I have changed the Maximum value from 100, its default value, to 1 so that the gauge will properly display the gross margin percentage. I also changed the scale values to percentage in the dialog box Number view and added a textbox. The resulting preview of the gauge is shown in Figure 3-53 indicating that the AdventureWorks Internet sales gross margin over all years is about 44 percent. If you change the parameter value in the upper right corner of the report to say 2008, the gauge pointer will move to the value for that year, and, of course, the matrix will be updated as well.

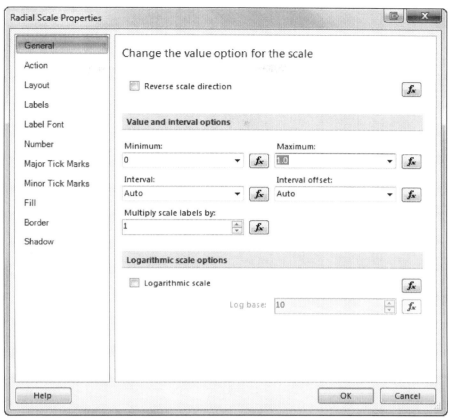

Figure 3-52 Scale Properties Dialog Box

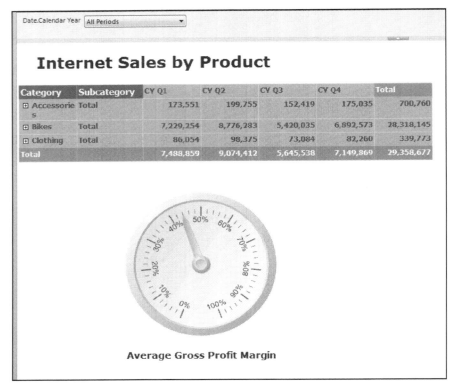

Figure 3-53 Completed Gauge Example Preview

Adding a List

A list is a type of free-form Tablix data region into which you can drop data fields, textboxes, etc. Figure 3-54 shows three stages of adding a list to our report. Here I have removed the matrix table and other items in the report that we inserted previously. A list is added to a report by clicking on List in the Insert tab and then drawing a rectangle on the design canvas. When you do that, a rectangle appears with a frame (container) around it with sizing handles. Clicking on the rectangle displays the list space shown by the top box in Figure 3-54. I also right clicked on the bar at the top to bring up the menu that is visible. In the list space shown in the middle of the figure I dropped four data fields: Calendar Quarter, Category, Subcategory, and Internet Sales Amount. If we preview the report at this point we will get page after page of quarter-category-subcategory-sales raw data. The bottom list space has the list formatted including adding page breaks to display each set of values on a separate page. A preview of the report with the list is shown in Figure 3-55. Note that only the bottom list in figure 3-54 is present in the actual report rdl file - I deleted the other two prior to running the report.

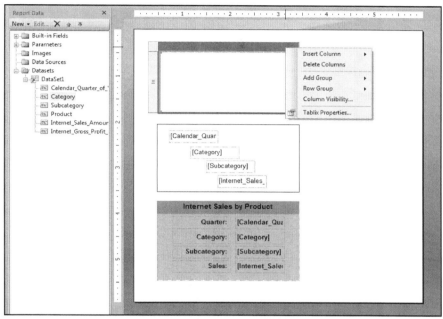

Figure 3-54 Adding a List to a Report

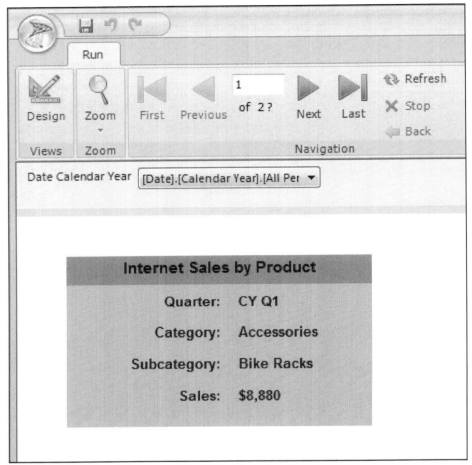

Figure 3-55 List in Preview

This list acts somewhat like a form in Visual Basic or Access with which you can scroll through individual records by clicking on the navigation buttons, the large arrow icons on the Ribbon. For example, clicking on Next will move to the next record: CY Q1, Accessories, Bike Stands. There are 633 pages (records) in the report for the combinations of quarter, categories, and subcategories.

Admittedly, this is a trivial example but it does demonstrate the potential for the List-type Tablix in a report. The List has additional functionality allowing it to serve as a container for other objects and grouped data. For example, you could incorporate a table and chart view in a listbox. Please see RB3 Help for more details.

Adding a Textbox, Image, Line, and Rectangle

The Insert tab in RB3 has four more sets of objects in addition to Data Regions: Data Visualizations, Report Items, Subreports, and Header & Footer. In Report Items double clicking on Text box, Line, or Rectangle adds that item to the report canvas. Double clicking on Image brings up the Image Properties dialog box shown in Figure 3-56 where you can name the image, create a tool tip, and select the file for the image from the General page. Images can be embedded in the report so that the report does not have to import them from an external source at the time the report is rendered. Or, you may use an external source by specifying a URL to it. You may also configure the image size, visibility, action, and border from the Image Properties dialog box. In this example I embedded the AdventureWorks Logo jpg into the report. Note that you use a similar process to add a background image to the body of a report or a Tablix, textbox, or rectangle in it.

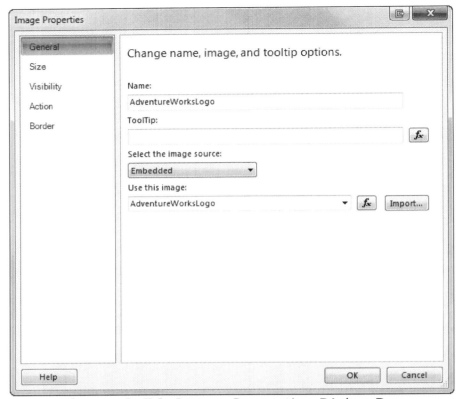

Figure 3-56 Image Properties Dialog Box

In Figure 3-57 I added a textbox, line, image and rectangle to the design surface and have selected all of them as indicated by the frames with sizing handles around them. The objects are formatted by right clicking on them, using the Properties panel on the right side of RB3, or using the formatting option on the Home tab. In the latter case, the formatting options on the Ribbon will enable only those options applicable to the type of object that you have selected. For example, when an image is selected only the Border formatting option is enabled.

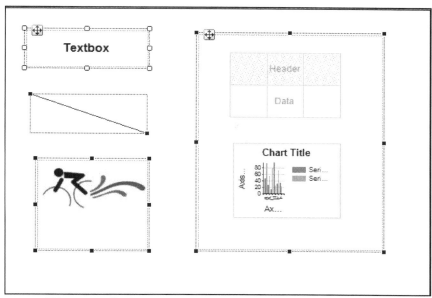

Figure 3-57 Image Properties Dialog Box

The rectangle, the object on the right side of Figure 3-55 acts as a container for other objects so that when the rectangle is moved the objects in it move with it. Here, I placed a table in the rectangle with a chart below it.

Adding Subreports and Page Headers and Footers

A subreport is just a separate report displayed inside the parent report. Both the report and its subreports are stored on the Report Server usually in the same folder. We saw an example of a subreport in Figure 1-9 and 1-10. You may pass parameters from the report to the subreport, and you may place a subreport in a Tablix data region.

We learned how to add headers and footers to a report in our discussion of Figure 3-38. Note that headers and footers here refer to page headers and footers and not to report headers and footers. When you display a report, headers and footers will be displayed on each page of the report. Report headers and footers are placed at the top and bottom of the report and appear only once at the top of the first page and the bottom of the last page of the report respectively.

Page headers and footers usually display something about the properties of the report or the page, e.g., page number, total pages, date, etc. For example, the report in Figure 3-30 includes a textbox holding a report execution datatime stamp.

Adding Key Performance Indicators (KPIs)

KPIs are metrics comparing actual performance with an objective and usually showing the trend of performance from the last period. More specifically with respect to Microsoft data analysis and data mining, a KPI is composed of a measure, its value, a goal and its degree of accomplishment, and a trend indicator. KPIs can be used in reports, dashboards and scorecards, Excel, or other places where you can access Analysis Services or create your own. For example, a convenience store operator may have a KPI for the gross margin on gasoline in cents per gallon, i.e., the difference between the selling price and cost, with an objective of at least $.15. The KPI in a report would present the current value of the margin, say $.12, its relationship with the goal - $.03 below, and its trend, say upward if the pervious margin was $.11.

Some KPIs that have already been created in the AdventureWorks cube include Growth in Customer Base, Net Income, and Operating Profit among others. For example, using the AdventureWorks cube data for the Product Gross Profit Margin KPI the Goal Expression in Multidimensional Expressions (MDX) but here provided in text defined the goal as:

> If the product category is Accessories, then the goal is .40 (40%)
> If the product category is Bikes, then the goal is .12 (12%)
> If the product category is Clothing, then the goal is .20 (20%)
> If the product category is Components, then the goal is .10 (10%)
> If the product category is anything else, then the goal is .12 (12 %%)

Using MDX the Status Expression creates a status value between 1 and -1, i.e., -1 <= Status Value <= 1, to indicate the degree of goal achievement as follows:

Status Value	Meaning
1	Very Good or High
.5	Good
0	Acceptable or Medium
-.5	Not So Good
-1	Bad or Low

The Status Expression for the example was written as:

If the KPI Value divided by the KPI Goal is greater than or equal to .90, then the Status Value is 1

If the KPI Value divided by the KPI Goal is less than .90 and greater than or equal to .80, then the Status Value is 0

If the KPI Value divided by the KPI Goal is anything else, then the Status Value is -1

The developer of this KPI choose not to use the intermediate status values of .5 and -.5.

So, suppose the gross profit margin for Accessories this period is .35 (35%), then the KPI Value divided by the KPI Goal would equal to .875 (.35 divided by .40 = .875), and, thus, the Status Value would be 0 or Acceptable.

The Status Value is represent visually by a Status indicator that is selected in the Status Indicator drop-down list which has Shapes selected for the Gross Profit Margin KPI. Other Status Indicator images in Reporting services using Visual Studio/BIDS are Cylinder, Traffic Light, Road Signs, Gauge, Reverse Gauge, Thermometer, Faces, and Variance Arrow. Most of these are not directly available in RB3.

Figure 3-58 shows a partial screen shot of an Excel pivot table that displays the data for the AdventureWorks Gross Profit Margin

KPI for each product category. Here the green circle represents a Status Value of 1 (very good); a yellow triangle represents a value of 0 (acceptable); and a red diamond represents a value of -1 (Bad). In 2006 Accessories only achieved 76.5% of the goal of 40% (30.6% divided by 40% = 76.5%) resulting in a Status Value of -1 with a red diamond indicator. Trend data may be represented in a similar manner.

	A	B	C	D	E	F
		Column Labels ▼				
Row Labels ▼		⊞ Accessories	⊞ Bikes	⊞ Clothing	⊞ Components	Grand Total
CY 2005						
Product Gross Profit Margin		40.4%	14.8%	-5.6%	8.8%	14.5%
Product Gross Profit Margin Goal		40.0%	12.0%	20.0%	10.0%	12.0%
Product Gross Profit Margin Status		◎	◎	◆	△	◎
CY 2006						
Product Gross Profit Margin		30.6%	9.1%	21.0%	11.8%	9.7%
Product Gross Profit Margin Goal		40.0%	12.0%	20.0%	10.0%	12.0%
Product Gross Profit Margin Status		◆	◆	◎	◎	△
CY 2007						
Product Gross Profit Margin		48.1%	8.7%	15.3%	7.6%	9.3%
Product Gross Profit Margin Goal		40.0%	12.0%	20.0%	10.0%	12.0%
Product Gross Profit Margin Status		◎	◆	◆	◆	◆
CY 2008						
Product Gross Profit Margin		55.2%	15.4%	19.4%	6.6%	15.6%
Product Gross Profit Margin Goal		40.0%	12.0%	20.0%	10.0%	12.0%
Product Gross Profit Margin Status		◎	◎	◎	◆	◎
CY 2010						
Product Gross Profit Margin						
Product Gross Profit Margin Goal		40.0%	12.0%	20.0%	10.0%	12.0%
Product Gross Profit Margin Status		◆	◆	◆	◆	◆
Total Product Gross Profit Margin		49.9%	11.1%	17.4%	8.8%	11.4%
Total Product Gross Profit Margin Goal		40.0%	12.0%	20.0%	10.0%	12.0%
Total Product Gross Profit Margin Status		◎	◎	△	△	◎

Figure 3-58 Key Performance Indicator Visualization Example

There are three ways to incorporate KPIs into a Report Builder report: by using background colors to represent different states of the KPI, by displaying the KPI on a gauge, and by using images to represent the KPI state. We use each approach in the next example. For the new report in Figure 3-59 I created a new dataset containing the Category dimension and the Gross Profit Margin KPI fields using the AdventureWorks Cube as the data source and created a calculated value for the percentage of goal accomplishment. I added a textbox at the top of the report, a table below it, and a gauge at the bottom. The table has product categories as rows and KPI values, goals, and status as columns, i.e., I dragged those fields from the Report Data list and dropped them onto the Tablix. The status value would normally not be visible but I included it here so that you could see it to compare the value to the visualization of it. For this example I ignored the KPI trend value but you treat it in the same way as we do the status value. The report in preview view after some tinkering is shown in Figure 3-60.

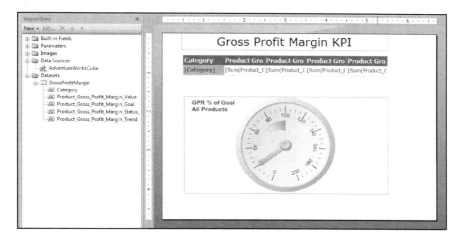

Figure 3-59 KPI Example in Design View

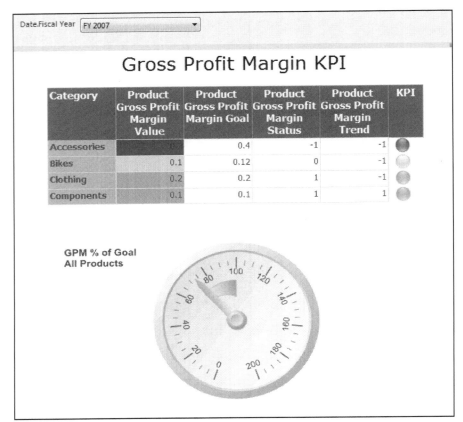

Figure 3-60 KPI Example in Preview View

Background Color Method

Recall from our discussion above that KPI status takes on values between -1 and +1 in 0.5 increments. Also recall that the Gross Profit Margin status value is determined as follows:

GPM KPI/GPM Goal	Status Value
>= .90	1
>= .80 and < .90	0
< .80	-1

Using an expression (which we'll discuss below) I set the

background fill color to green, yellow, and red for the status values of 1, 0, and -1 respectively as is shown in the figure. Neat!

Gauge Method

The gauge also uses an expression to determine its pointer value as a percentage:

= GPM KPI/GPM Goal*100

I set the gauge scale maximum to 200 (percent) because the KPI can exceed its goal, set the scale font to bold, and added a label in the upper right corner.

Image Method

To use images to represent KPI values I added the column on the right side of the table titled KPI and then added an expression in Image Properties where it says "Use this image" (Figure 3-56) with reference to images of colored balls to represent the different status values. Prior to that I added three images to the report as shown in Figure 3-61. To add an image to Report Data right click on Images which will bring up a file Open dialog box and proceed from there as usual.

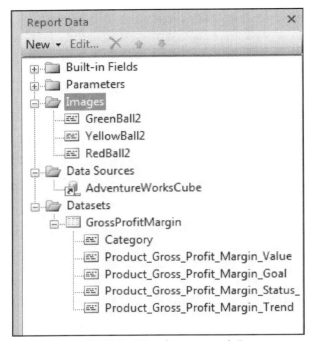

Figure 3-61 Background Images

Using Expressions and Built-in Fields

Expressions provide great flexibility in the design of a report. As you saw above we used expressions to set colors and images for KPI values. We can also use them to perform calculations, filter values, format data and objects, and so on.

To create or modify an expression click on the **fx** button (there are two in Figure 3-56) to bring up the Expression dialog box. The Expression dialog box for the gauge in Figure 3-59 is shown in Figure 3-60. All expressions begin with an equal symbol. You may write the expression manually but it's far easier to use category items to build it. For example, the fields available in the GrossProfitMargin dataset are listed in the Values listbox in Figure 3-62. I double clicked on the GPM Value field to insert it into the expression, added the divide operator, double clicked on the GPM Goal field, and added the multiplication operator and the number 100 to complete the expression.

The Category panel lists items that are commonly used in expressions. Constants, Parameters, and Variables list the ones available in the report. In our case there are no constants or variables but there would be if we had created them. DateCalendarYear would be listed as the only parameter. Built-in Fields, the same ones as in the Report Data panel for this report shown on the left side of Figure 3-59, are listed in Figure 3-63a. This list contains global and user variables for the report which are usually used in headers and footers. For example, the crude report in Figure 3-41 uses the ExecutionTime built-in field to display the datetime that the report is run. Similarly, you may use the PageNumber and TotalPages fields to print "Page X of Y Pages" in a footer.

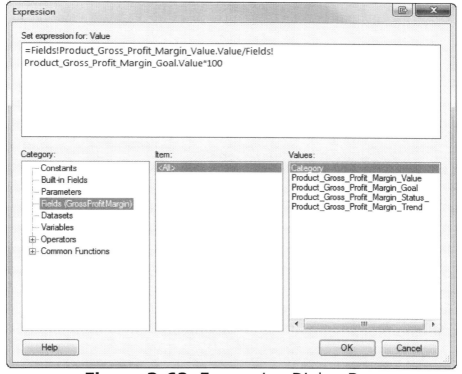

Figure 3-62 Expression Dialog Box

The Fields and Datasets categories list the ones available in the report. (The fields are shown in the figure above.) Operators lists the usual computer programming arithmetic, comparison, concatenation, and logical operators, in this case from Visual

Basic. Common functions provide a number of categories of Visual Basic functions available as in Figure 3-63b where some of the date and time functions are displayed in the Item pane. Again, all you have to do to add one of the items to the expression is to double click on it.

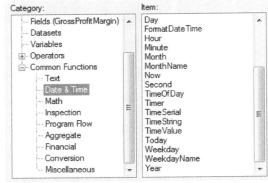

Figure 3-63a Build-in Fields   **Figure 3-63b** Common Functions

Figure 3-63 Expression Category Examples

If you are interested in the expression for the background color of the Product Gross Profit margin Value column in Figure 3-58, it uses the IIF function:

```
=IIF(Fields!Product_Gross_Profit_Margin_Status
    _.Value>=1, "Lime",
  IIF(Fields!Product_Gross_Profit_Margin_Status
    _.Value=0,"Yellow", "Red"))
```

Note that for this expression the Constants category presents a color picker in the Values pane so all I had to do to set the color for a status value was to click the color. The expression for the background image for the KPI column also uses a similar IIF function:

```
=IIF(Fields!Product_Gross_Profit_Margin_Status_.Value>=
    1, "GreenBall2",
  IIF(Fields!Product_Gross_Profit_Margin_Status_.Value=0,"
    YellowBall2", "RedBall2"))
```

To use custom code like the ChangeWord function example

presented earlier use an expression something like:
=Code.ChangeWord(<reference to word to change>). Please see
Report Builder 3.0 Help for more examples of expressions.

Adding Databars, Sparklines, and Indicators

Databars and sparklines are small charts and indicators are small
gauges without elements such as pointers. There are five types of
sparklines: column charts, line charts, area charts, pie charts, and
range charts. Databars are horizontal or vertical bars showing
some sort of value(s). Indicators are used to display a single
value such as the status of a KPI. There are four indicator image
types: directional that show trend direction, symbols such as
checkmarks and flags, shapes like the balls we used in Figure 3-
58, and ratings such as stars, bars, and pie charts.

You add one of these objects to a report by clicking on it on the
RB3 Insert ribbon and then clicking in the cell destination. For
example, in a new report using the InternetSales dataset that we
used previously I inserted four tables as shown in Figure 3-64. All
use internet sales as the row field. The first, second, and fourth
table use calendar year as the column field, and the third uses
calendar quarter. I added a second column to each table to
display the data visualization. You must manually enter the
heading on that column.

After inserting the object you specify its data in a manner similar
to what we used with gauges in Figure 3-51 by dragging a data
item from the Report Data pane into the data drop-down box as
shown in Figure 3-65a. This menu is displayed by clicking on the
cell containing the object. The objects can be modified by using
drop-down menus as displayed in Figure 3-65b by right clicking on
the cell containing the object. Figure 3-66 shows the resultant
report. Note that I used different sparklines for the second and
third tables: a line chart for the second and a bar chart for the
third.

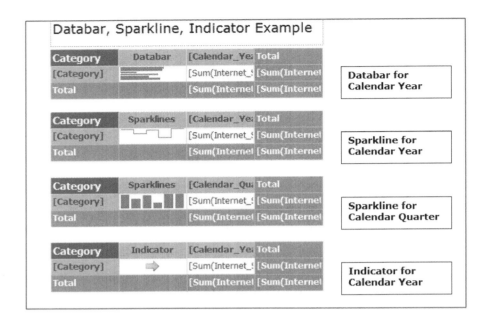

Figure 3-64 Databar, Sparkline, and Indicator Design Example

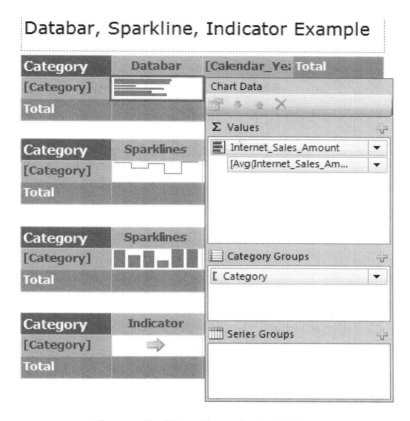

Figure 3-65a Chart Data Options

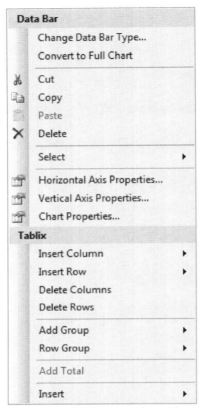

Figure 3-65b Databar Menu

Figure 3-65 Databar, Sparkline, and Indicator Design
Example

Databar, Sparkline, Indicator Example

Category	Databar	CY 2005	CY 2006	CY 2007	CY 2008	Total
Accessories				293,710	407,050	700,760
Bikes		3,266,374	6,530,344	9,359,103	9,162,325	28,318,145
Clothing				138,248	201,525	339,773
Total		3,266,374	6,530,344	9,791,060	9,770,900	29,358,677

Category	Sparklines	CY 2005	CY 2006	CY 2007	CY 2008	Total
Accessories				293,710	407,050	700,760
Bikes		3,266,374	6,530,344	9,359,103	9,162,325	28,318,145
Clothing				138,248	201,525	339,773
Total		3,266,374	6,530,344	9,791,060	9,770,900	29,358,677

Category	Sparklines	CY Q1	CY Q2	CY Q3	CY Q4	Total
Accessories		173,551	199,755	152,419	175,035	700759.96
Bikes		7,229,254	8,776,283	5,420,035	6,892,573	28318144.65 07
Clothing		86,054	98,375	73,084	82,260	339772.61
Total		7488858.712 7	9074412.342 2	5645537.612 4	7149868.553 4	29358677.22 07

Category	Indicator	CY 2005	CY 2006	CY 2007	CY 2008	Total
Accessories	↓			293,710	407,050	700,760
Bikes	↑	3,266,374	6,530,344	9,359,103	9,162,325	28,318,145
Clothing	↓			138,248	201,525	339,773
Total		3,266,374	6,530,344	9,791,060	9,770,900	29,358,677

Figure 3-66 Databar, Sparkline, and Indicator Report

Instead of importing images for KPI visualization as we did in Figure 3-58 we could use indicators as shown in Figure 3-67. In design view I dropped an indicator object into the KPI value cell, selected the three color shapes type, and specified the value in the Value and States window of the Indicator Properties menu shown in Figure 3-68. In this case the value is [Sum(Product_Gross_Profit_Margin_Status_)] showing the trend of the Gross Profit Margin.

Using sparklines and indicators in Excel is addressed in the full version of my BI book.

Gross Profit Margin KPI

Category	Product Gross Profit Margin Value	Product Gross Profit Margin Goal	Product Gross Profit Margin Status	Product Gross Profit Margin Trend	KPI
Accessories		0.4	-1	-1	●
Bikes	0.1	0.12	0	-1	◐
Clothing	0.2	0.2	1	-1	●
Components	0.1	0.1	1	1	●

Figure 3-67 KPI with Indicators

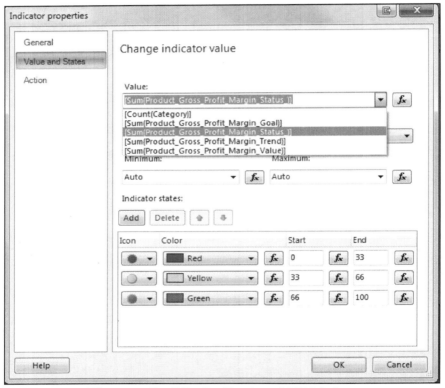

Figure 3-68 Indicator KPI Value

Adding Maps

RB3 can overlay data visualizations on geographical maps. These maps require both analytical data (values) and spatial data (locations). There are four sources for spatial data: the Map Gallery installed with RB3 that uses U.S. Census Bureau data; Environmental Systems Research Institute (ESRI) Shapefiles with geographic information in a vector data format; spatial data stored in a SQL Server database (see SQL Server Books Online); and custom locations created by the user(see RB3 Help). We do not have space for complete coverage of RB3 maps so I will only describe a simple example here, a map of the United States showing the value of AdventureWorks internet sales by state.

It's relatively easy to design maps using the Map Wizard. In design view click new in the Report Builder button menu and then select the Map Wizard. This will bring you to the New Map page in Figure 3-69a where there are three types of spatial data to choose from. We will use the Map Gallery that has maps for the United States. Within the Map Gallery I selected US by State Insert to select the type of map to use.

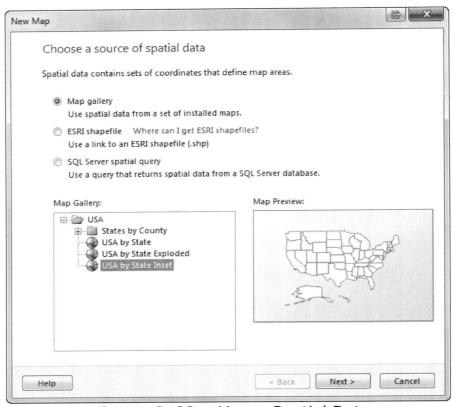

Figure 3-69a Map – Spatial Data

Clicking Next will take you to a page (Figure 3-67b) to select view options where you may use the directional arrows to change the shape of the map. I did not use the Bing Map Layer that lets you add roads and /or aerial views to the map. The next page shown in Figure 3-67c provides three map types: Basic, Color, and Bubble. I choose the Color Analytical Map.

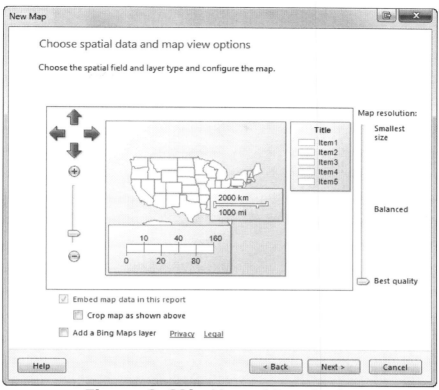

Figure 3-69b Map – View Options

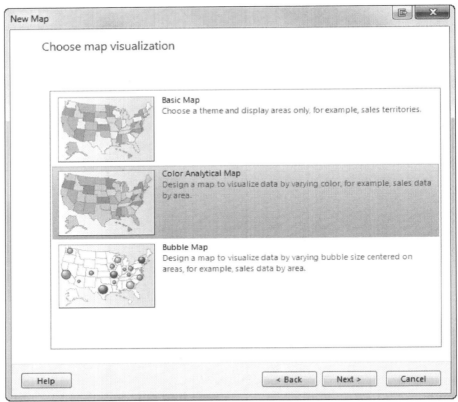

Figure 3-69c Map – Visualization Type

You specify the analytical dataset, the data to be overplayed on the map, in the next window (Figure 3-69d). Here you choose between an existing dataset or one that you will add. I choose add a dataset so I could construct the query for the map data. Clicking Next takes you to a data source page (Figure 3-69e) that you are familiar with. I selected the AdventureWorks Cube. Next in the Query Designer (Figure 3-69f) I dragged Internet Sales Amount from the Measures group and State-Province from the Customer Geography Fact list onto the design surface and Country and Calendar Year into the filter area. I selected United States for the Filter Expression for Country to only use US sales data and marked the Calendar Year filter as a parameter so that the user could select what data to display on the map. Note that you could also add a calendar quarter parameter to be able select quarters as well as years.

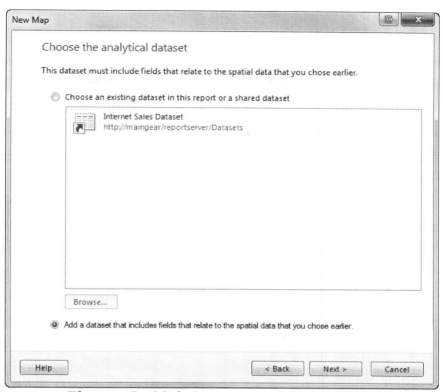

Figure 3-69d Map – Analytical Dataset

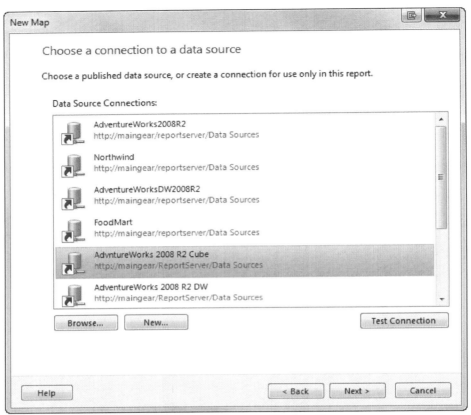

Figure 3-69e Map – Data Source

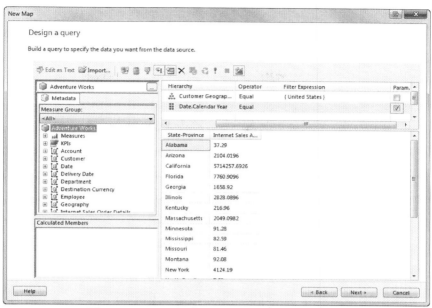

Figure 3-69f Map – Query Design

In the next window (Figure 3-69g) you match spatial and analytical data fields. In this case the spatial data are in the STATENAME field and the analytical data are in the State Province field.

Figure 3-69g Map – Field Match

Next you choose the theme, data field to use, and the color rule for the map in Figure 3-69h. I left the theme at the default (Ocean); selected [Sum(Internet_Sales_Amount)] for the data to display, i.e., data will be summed for each state; and the Light-Dark color rule where states with lower internet sales will be show lighter and those with higher sales will be darker. You can see in the drop-down list that there are a number of color combinations.

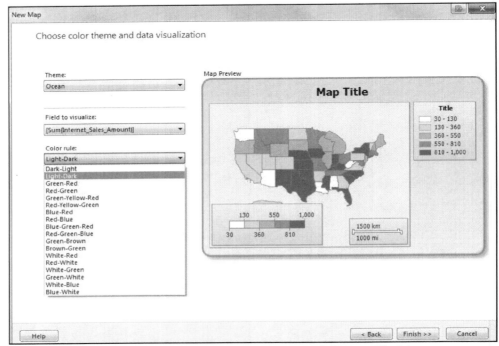

Figure 3-69h Map – Theme and Data Field

Figure 3-69i shows the completed map in design view, and Figure 3-69j the run view. In the run view it's obvious the AdventureWorks' sales are predominately on the West Coast something that AW's marketing department may want to investigate. Note that by changing map parameter values (not shown), i.e., changing years and/or quarters, the sales pattern change over time. Interesting.

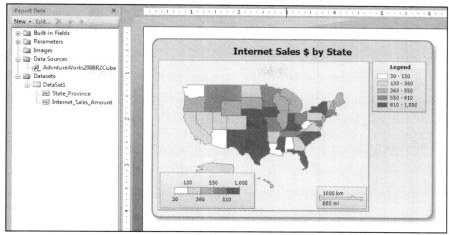

Figure 3-69i Map – Design View

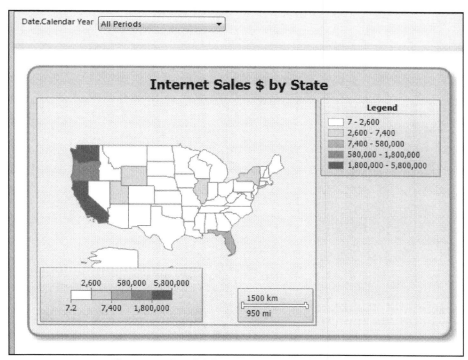

Figure 3-69j Map – Run View

Using Actions

Some report objects have Action as a property category along with General, Number, Font, Visibility, etc. Actions are essentially hyperlinks, i.e., clicking on an object with a defined action will navigate to the action's target: another report on the Report Sever, a bookmark, or hyperlink. You may create actions for textboxes, including those in a Tablix, images, and maps. Figure 3-70 shows the action view for a Textbox Properties dialog box in which I specified the Gross Profit Margin KPI report we worked on above as the action target. That report already has a calendar year parameter so I did not add one here.

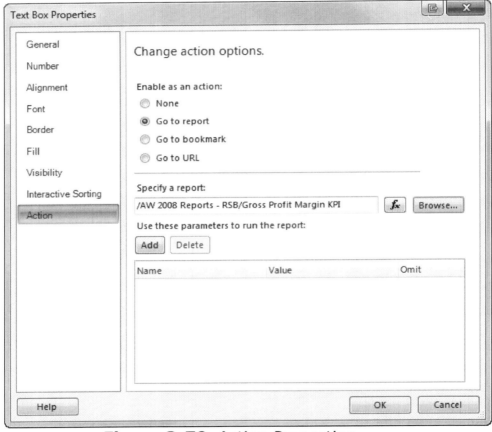

Figure 3-70 Action Properties

As an example the report in Figure 3-71 shows the report from Figure 3-43 with a textbox and image added to it, both of which have actions specified in them. The textbox "Go to KPI Report" uses the action defined in Figure 3-70 to navigate to the GPM KPI report. Note that a report specified in an action must be already published to the Report Server. The action for the Microsoft image is set to a hyperlink to the Microsoft home page. So, when the report is run, clicking on the KPI Report textbox will take you to that report and clicking on the Microsoft image will bring up the Microsoft home page in your default browser.

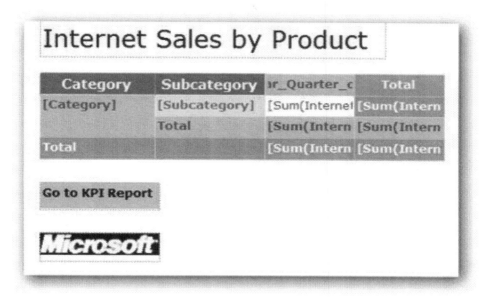

Figure 3-71 Action Example

You add an Action to an object by right clicking on the object to display the Properties dialog box, selecting Action and the Action type, and then specifying the target in the textbox provided.

Drill-through, Drill-down, Subreports, and Nested Data Regions

A drill-through report displays another report when the user clicks on a specific textbox in the parent report. For example, in the Internet Sales by Product report in Figure 3-69 I could right click on the [Subcategory] cell to bring up the Properties window and then proceed to define an Action to go to another report. Then, when the report runs and the user clicks on that cell, the other report will be displayed. A subreport is similar to a drill-through report except that the other report is displayed within the parent report.

The Internet Sales by Product report in Figure 3-43 has the drill-down capability whereby a dimension can be expanded to show the underlying detail as Accessories are expanded in the Figure to display product subcategories.

Similarly, nested data regions display other data regions, say a sub-table, or a data visualization, say an indicator, within another data region. The Gross Profit Margin KPI report in Figure 3-58 is an example where the KPI is nested within the GPM table. Please see RB3 Help for more information about these topics.

Publishing Reports to the Report Server

As mentioned earlier reports are saved with an rdl file extension either to a storage device such as your local hard drive or to the Report Server or to both. If you save reports in both places, be aware that a changed report saved to one location does not automatically update the other version, i.e., the new version must be saved in both locations.

To publish a report to the report server that has not been saved there before either save it from RB3 to the Report Server or upload the file from the storage location by using the Report Manager. We addressed uploading earlier in this chapter. To save the file from RB3 to the Report Server click on Save As from the list displayed when clicking the RB3 button in the upper left corner to bring up the Save As Report dialog box shown in Figure 3-72. Select Recent Sites and Servers on the left and double click on the server URL in the right panel to list the folders available on the Server. Select a folder and then save the file. To save the report to a new folder either use Report Manager to create it prior to saving the report from RB3 or save it to an existing Server folder temporarily and then use the Report manager to create the new folder and move the report to it. Of course, you may change the file name of the report to how you want it to appear on the Server by entering the new name in the Name box or renaming it within the Report Manager.

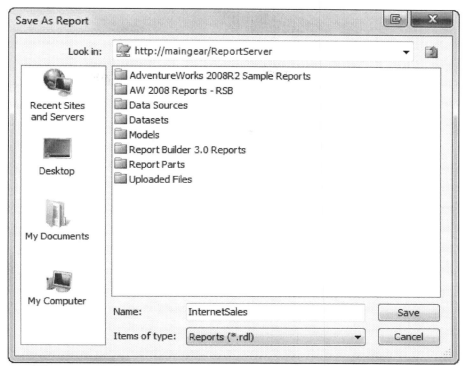

Figure 3-72 Save a Report to the Report Server

I published most of the reports that we used as examples in this chapter to my report server's AW 2008 Reports - RSB folder shown in Figure 3-73. Note that I changed the names of the reports to something more descriptive. After publishing the report to the Report Server, I would probably rename the locally stored version as well and include a version number in the name for backup purposes.

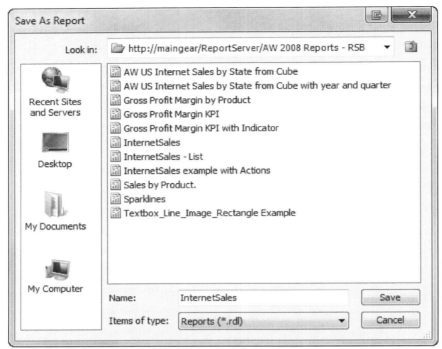

Figure 3-73 Reports on the Report Server

The Report Part Gallery

Report parts are report objects such as tables, charts, and images saved on the report server that can be used in other reports. You save report parts in RB3 by clicking on the RB button in the upper left corner to display the drop-down menu as in Figure 3-74. Clicking the Publish Report Parts button will bring up the window in Figure 3-75 where you select the setting to use for the parts. To publish all objects as is with default settings select the top option. To modify the properties select the bottom option that will take you to the Select report parts to publish window as in Figure 3-76 where you can select which reports and datasets to publish.

Figure 3-74 Action Example

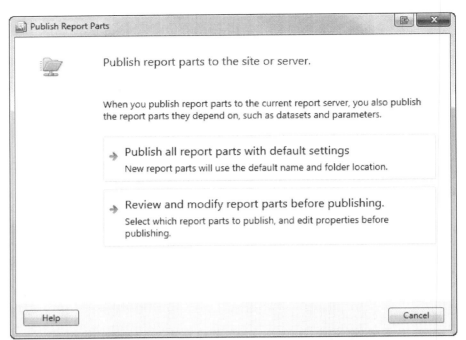

Figure 3-75 Report Parts Publish Options

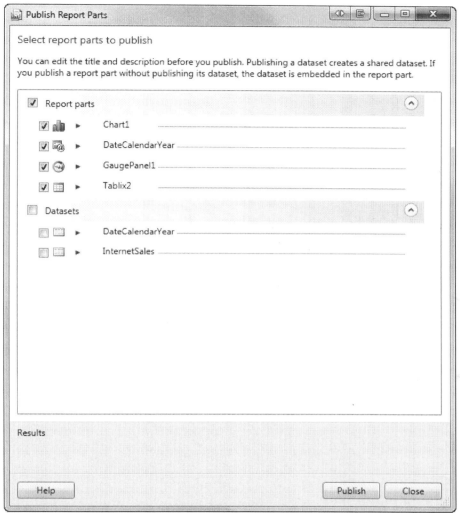

Figure 3-76 Review and Modify Report Parts Window

The report parts will be published (saved) on the report server to the folder specified in the Report Builder Options window accessed from the RB3 button in the top left corner. I left the folder set to the default (Report Parts) where I saved objects from some of the reports we used earlier. Figure 3-77 shows the objects in the Maingear/Report Server/Report Parts folder which are also displayed in the Report Part Gallery on the right edge of the RB3 window as in Figure 3-78. In that Gallery you can specify search criteria such as created, modified, and type and set the server folder to search. Note that you must click on the magnifying glass button in the upper right corner to display a list of objects. To use an object in a report you may either drag and drop it the from the Gallery onto the design surface or double click it. Using RB3's report parts capability can significantly reduce report design time.

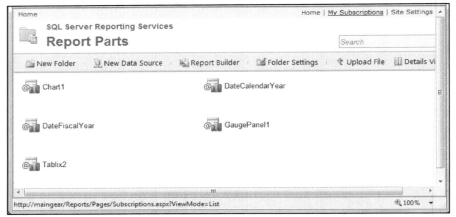

Figure 3-77 Report Parts Folder

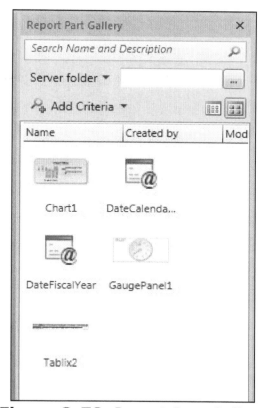

Figure 3-78 Report Part Gallery

We have most definitively not covered all of the features of the Report Manager and especially of Report Builder 3.0, and for RB3 we have slighted some of the topics that we addressed so please see Books Online, RB3 Help, or other sources for coverage of more advanced topics.

This concludes this introduction to Microsoft Report Builder and Report Manager. If you have an interest in Microsoft Business Intelligence tools that you may use within Excel and/or Access, please see my BI Book (http://www.zerobits.info/report-builder-book/) whose chapter titles are listed below (another obvious plug).

Chapter 1   Introduction
Chapter 2   Business Intelligence Overview

Thanks for reading this book.

About the Author

Robert S. "Bob" Bussom retired early from academia where he served as a professor and administrator. He has other work experience in retail sales, heavy manufacturing, health insurance, and executive development. He earned a B.S., MBA, and Ph. D. from The Ohio State University and has additional graduate-level coursework in Information Systems.

Made in the USA
Lexington, KY
26 August 2013